EPISODES:
Texas Dow
1940 - 1976

The publication of this
SPECIAL LIMITED EDITION
is sponsored by
THE LAKE JACKSON HISTORICAL ASSOCIATION

THIS IS COPY # 408

OF THE 1600 COPIES

IN THIS

SPECIAL LIMITED EDITION

EPISODES:
TEXAS DOW
1940 - 1976

Bill Colegrove

LARKSDALE
HOUSTON

SPECIAL LIMITED EDITION

EPISODES: TEXAS DOW 1940 - 1976

Copyright 1989 by William Colegrove

First printing April 1983; adapted from a series of feature articles by Bill Colegrove, published in 1981 and 1982 in the BRAZOSPORT FACTS, Lake Jackson, Texas.

ISBN 0-89896-073-8

Book Design, Frances Burke Goodman
Production Coordinators, A. Lee Chichester and
    Kathleen Carbone
Technical Coordinator, Mohsen Khorsandian
Mechanical Production, Hamid Arjomandnia

LARKSDALE
HOUSTON

Printed and manufactured by LARKSDALE, in the United States of America.

ACKNOWLEDGMENT

I want to acknowledge the wonderful support and help given me by so many people in the Dow organization including Mr. H. H. McClure, the present General Manager of the Texas Division. Also I want to thank Jim Nabors, publisher of the *Brazosport Facts*; Glenn Heath, executive editor of the *Facts*, as well as my longtime editor of this and a former series of columns, Roberta Dansby of the *Brazosport Facts*.

Also, to Sena, my wife, who gave me inspiration and then insisted on a high standard of excellence in my writing.

INTRODUCTION

This book really began in 1976, when Bill Colegrove was asked to do a history of Texas Dow from its beginning in late 1939 through the year 1976.

The job was made easier because he was at Texas Dow from 1940, working for several years as secretary to Dr. A. P. Beutel, General Manager of Dow's Texas Division.

During the early 40s he saw what took place, and in 1976 interviewed people in Dow and outside of Dow in the community, who helped make the events he wrote about.

In the late summer of 1981, Jim Nabors, publisher of the *Brazosport Facts*, read the history which had been written in 1976, and believed this material should be expanded and run as a weekly series of articles in the *Brazosport Facts*. Nabors thought if it were dished up piece-meal, many people would read and enjoy it.

What followed was 48 weekly articles, complete with pictures, which ran in the *Facts* as "Episodes—Texas Dow 1940-76." So many readers of the column requested it be put in book form, that this book is the answer to the requests.

Bill has had a close association with Dow's hotel, cafeterias, hospital, trailer park, and with Dow Houses, Camp Chemical, Dow Lodge, Brazoria Reservoir and other facilities.

He was also mayor of Lake Jackson six years during its formative stage, and was connected with many community activities such as Red Cross, County Fair, bond drives, Community Chest, United Fund, Welfare Planning Council, Youth Employment, Junior Achievement, Beautify Texas Council and many others.

All this makes him uniquely qualified to record for all of us

7

the history of Brazosport and Texas Dow from the late 1930s through 1976.

Bill says he wrote these columns to give the flavor of the community, the people, the interesting life styles, and to show how one chemical industry under a most unusual leader, Dr. A. P. Beutel, intertwined the growth of the industry with the growth and changes in the local community.

The columns each stand alone, although they follow a general time trail from 1940 through 1976.

TABLE OF CONTENTS

EPISODES:
Texas Dow
1940 - 1976

1

Fishing Village To Frontier Town

THE COMING of the Dow Chemical Co. to Freeport in 1940 changed this sleepy little fishing village of 3,500 people into a big, rough, frontier town, with all the loud clamor of more than 10,000 construction workers. Suddenly, people were almost crawling over each other, as the temporary buildings popped out of the ground to be replaced in days by semi-permanent and permanent structures.

I saw it all. I remember a lazy summer day in 1940, when I walked down a quiet main street in what was then Velasco, and saw not a single person on the street, not even a dog or a cat. Then one night in 1942, there were 10,000 construction workers busy around the clock at Plant B, and the night was lit up with floodlights like Broadway and 42nd Street.

Reviewing what happened to Mrs. W. E. Clark's rooming and boarding house gives one a bit of perspective. Before the milling crowds swarmed into Freeport, she had a few Freeport Sulphur Company engineers and some school teachers—about 20 people. Then came Dow and the construction people with no place to live. Workers even slept on the floor at the boarding house just to get away from the mosquitoes. Mrs. Clark was soon feeding up to 200 every meal, putting them at long tables in shifts.

At the beginning, just 85 rooms were available in Freeport. There were also 25 rooms at the Tarpon Inn where the officials of Dow and Austin Company, the general contractor for plant construction, stayed.

Before Dow arrived on the scene, Freeport was a cigar-shaped city with a nine-hole golf course on the west end, and Stauffer Chemical Company on the east end. Development ended with Fourth Street.

The Freeport Theater on Second Street was the only movie house. Most of the business area consisted of vacant lots, which enticed youngsters with baseballs and bats for sandlot games. Shortly after dark each night, the street lights were extinguished. There were no sidewalks on Second Street. You walked on planks.

Velasco had a few houses on Avenues A and B, plus a few businesses on Avenue A. There were a couple of store buildings and a half dozen scattered houses in Clute.

The Sulphur Company had curtailed operations in 1935, thus eliminating some jobs.

About December 1939, there were rumors of a chemical company coming to Freeport. There was a Sulphur Company chemist staying at the Tarpon Inn taking water samples, but no one knew who they were for. Raymond Walker said it was a pretty well-kept secret.

One morning in May of 1940, Dr. A. P. Beutel got together with Neil Warren, an architect, over a cup of coffee. "We need a hotel," said Beutel, "in a hurry." Warren pulled out a scratch pad and scribbled down the layout of a 23-room hotel. Dr. Beutel looked at it and nodded. At 2 p.m. that day, Howard Cox, of Austin Company Purchasing, asked C. W. Vetterling to check a load of lumber for the new Dow Hotel.

The hotel was built in three weeks, from notebooks and field sketches, and was opened for business. Raymond Walker, the first resident manager, said the hotel was unique in those days because each room had a bath. There was also a uniformed porter and a 24-hour clerk on duty.

One day, many years later, I was hotel manager and wanted to do some remodeling. There were no blueprints—we had to measure everything on the ground and make blueprints to start the remodeling.

BUILT QUICKLY—The Dow Hotel, much later renamed the Freeport Inn, looked like this in 1940 when it was built in three weeks time to provide badly needed housing for the hundreds of people crowding into town then.

HOTEL MANAGER- Raymond Walker was assistant manager of the Tarpon Inn when Dow moved into Texas. He later became the first resident manager of the Dow Hotel. Walker retired from Dow in September 1978 and still lives in Lake Jackson.

THE FREEPORT FACTS

FREEPORT, TEXAS, THURSDAY, MARCH 7, 1940

Brazoria County's Most Complete Newspaper

VOL. 27, NO. 49—Established 1913

DOW CHEMICAL CO. WILL PURCHASE 800-ACRE SITE ON FREEPORT HARBOR

At a meeting of the board of directors of the Dow Chemical Company of Midland, Michigan, scheduled for this morning (Thursday) the concern, one of the largest chemical companies of the United States, expects to authorize the purchase of approximately 800 acres of land bordering on Freeport Harbor to be used as a site for the location of a chemical plant.

This acreage will give the company approximately three miles of harbor frontage in the big bend of the channel on the Velasco side of the river. The company has had an option on this acreage for a number of months.

Dow Chemical Company is a several million dollar concern.

This is the good news residents of Freeport, Velasco and this section have awaited eagerly since the company became interested in a location here almost a year ago. Board of directors

Telegram Received At 8:00 A. M. Today

Midland, Mich., Mar. 6, 1940.

Editor Freeport Facts
Freeport, Tex.

Answering your wire wish to advise that at a meeting of board of directors of the Dow Chemical Company to be held on Thursday morning, March Seventh we expect to authorize the purchase of approximately 800 acres of land from the Freeport Sulphur Company having approximately three miles of harbor frontage. We expect to proceed with construction of a plant if a number of contracts now pending can be satisfactorily concluded. Regret cannot give you further information until plans are more definitely outlined.

Willard H. Dow, president,
The Dow Chemical Co.

here was received Tuesday of this week by The Facts in a telegram from Willard H. Dow, president of the company, expressing the desire to make a statement today.

Establishment of the plant here is expected to provide the spark that will bring Freeport harbor into its own and encourage other development and expansion along its many other miles of available and desirable frontage.

Although the main plant of the Dow Company is located at Midland, Michigan, the firm has branches at many other points throughout the country.

The company manufactures over two hundred different types of chemical products and its markets extend throughout the world.

Officials and directors of the company during their several visits to Freeport have impressed local people with their general exce

BIGGEST HEADLINE-Dow's coming, announced in this March 7, 1940, edition, accounted for the biggest headline for The Freeport Facts, then a 27-year-old

2

Dow's Coming Here
Tied To World War II

IF WE look back a moment to see why Dow Chemical Co. came to Freeport when it did, we will learn that World War II and Dow's Texas Division were closely associated. However, even before Hitler invaded Poland on September 2, 1939, to start World War II, Dow's president, Willard Dow, and his top management could see it coming.

They had decided to expand into Texas with a chemical complex to produce the basic chemicals they knew would be needed. During the summer and early fall of 1939, they were studying sites along the Gulf Coast which earlier exploratory work had shown to be good prospects for chemical products.

Corpus Christi fought hard for this Dow plant. In the Michigan office of Dr. A. P. Beutel, who was to become the Texas Division's first general manager, I recall seeing the beautiful brochures on all the advantages Corpus Christi said they would offer.

Freeport was finally chosen because of the following conditions which were not met anywhere else in all the world:

1. Seawater at 100 percent salinity, with 10 pounds of magnesium and one-half pound of bromine in each 1,000

gallons of seawater.

2. 15 percent of the nation's proven reserves of natural gas within a 100-mile radius.

3. Salt domes within 15 miles.

4. Oyster shell for lime only 45 to 75 miles away.

5. Sulphur nearby.

6. A harbor that could be reached by all but the largest ocean-going vessels.

7. Intracoastal canal right at the site.

8. Salt water from the Old Brazos River and waste water to the New Brazos River gave a 15-mile separation to prevent dilution.

Dow bought an 823-acre site in Freeport for their plant on March 7, 1940, and announced on March 13 they would build a 10-million-pound per year magnesium plant for $5 million. The Austin Company would do the engineering and construction of the plant.

On March 15, 1940, Harland Sherbrook arrived on the scene at Freeport. He was Dow's construction superintendent in charge of building all the Freeport plants, most of which were built during World War II. Sherbrook, now deceased, was given credit by the late Dr. Beutel for getting Plants A and B built in an incredibly short time despite a most difficult war-time shortage of materials and manpower.

By March 20, carpenters had begun work on a temporary office for Dow and Austin Company, and completed it in two days. Seven days later, trucks began hauling fill for the permanent office building, A-1201. On March 29, Dow and Austin Company moved into their permanent building.

The first carload of construction equipment arrived at Velasco (now North Freeport) on March 22, but there was no railroad track to the plant site. The railroad crew worked all day Easter Sunday, and the railroad was completed by Monday morning.

Then in April of 1940, a group of Dow engineers under George Greene started commuting from Midland, Michigan, to Cleveland, Ohio, where some 300 Austin Company engineers went to work on the design of the Freeport plants.

Gerry Reichenbach, a Midland Dow engineer, told about the

Cleveland job. After working all week in Cleveland, including several nights each week till 10 p.m., they would leave the office at 7 or 8 p.m. on Friday and go to the D. and C. boat docks, where they put their car on the D. and C. ferry, and got a stateroom for the overnight trip to Detroit. A bar on the ship was conveniently open all night. From Detroit, they drove to Midland, arriving there about noon on Saturday.

Burt Haas also tells of commuting by train to Cleveland. They drove from Midland to Saginaw, took the Pere Marquette train to Detroit, then the Michigan Central to Cleveland. The Michigan Central was a special high-speed train.

Burt remembers one trip when the high-speed train hit an automobile just after the driver managed to get out. They scattered Fuller Brush order forms for about five miles.

H A R L A N D S H E R B R O O K — He was credited with getting the first plants built in record time despite wartime shortages.

BURT HAAS — He was an engineer at Dow Chemical, Midland, Mich. He came to Texas with Dow, married here and Lake Jackson Farms is now his retirement home.

KIBITZER—In 1940 when Dow's Texas Division plants began to rise out of the saltgrass, goats like this one were roaming the area and often watched the construction taking away their pasture land.

3

Many Workers
Lived At Plant Site

IVAN ODEN was in charge of construction and operation auditing. He was the first Dow Chemical Co. executive to stay in Freeport as the construction of the Texas Division began. He set up office in an abandoned furniture store during March of 1940.

Oden said he saw the biggest cockroaches he had ever seen in his life. At one of the local cafes, he saw a giant cockroach crawling behind the cereal boxes. The roach was so big it stuck out at both ends of the cereal box.

Oden thought he had been sent to Siberia.

For entertainment in those days, there was Buck's Hall in Brazoria, a large dance hall where big bands played. Other hot spots were Palacios, Sylvan Beach near Houston, the Hollywood Dinner Club in Galveston, and Peck Kelly at the Southern Dinner Club in Houston. On Bryan Beach, there was a big concrete dance floor with palms planted all around the sides. Big bands played there, including Phil Harris.

Many people here would go to Houston for the weekend. It was about a two-hour drive each way over very poor roads, but the city had a lot of entertainment.

In April, Dow had a six-unit apartment house under

construction in Freeport. By May, the 23-room hotel was built.

Also in May, Dow purchased 800 more acres adjacent to Plant A, making a total of 1,623 acres. During the summer of 1940, work was started on the Ethyl Dow bromine plant adjacent to the Dow Plant A site.

John Stark, of Dow's Construction Purchasing Department, tells of the great quantities of materials needed for construction. For instance, at the Ethyl Dow plant, lath came by the bargeload, and millions of bricks were brought in by freight cars.

Many materials for Plant A construction, such as bricks, roofing, etc., were field purchased. Vendors from Houston would come down, and sitting at school desks in the halls by the purchasing office, they would study the blueprints, figure the quantity and quote on the spot. After checking quantities and prices, the vendors would be given a field order right there. They couldn't wait.

Meanwhile at the plant site, several Pullman cars had been moved in to give some of the workers a place to sleep. Also, for a short time, there was a ship tied near the old abandoned warehouse on the Plant A peninsula, where workers slept in staterooms.

Soon, however, barracks and a mess hall were built to house and feed the workers. Bill Roper, a longtime member of Dow security, tells about the facilities.

They were built about where Chlorine 5 is located now. The accompanying picture shows the three long barracks buildings, and the mess hall across the service road. The V-shaped A-2401 office and the first shop buildings are shown in the background on the peninsula.

The barracks rooms each had a three-quarter bed, a closet and a gas heater.

Some memories include home-cooked food the men would fix on a stove they installed in a washroom. Nearly all were hunters and fishermen. Roper killed an 8-point buck one time, strung him up above the big drain in the washroom and skinned him. They ate off that buck for several days, then put the rest in a stew.

The mess hall served "family style" on big tables with benches. Platters of food would be placed on the tables and then there would be a wild grab by hungry construction workers.

I ate there several times and thought the food was good. At one point, the mess hall workers raised their own chickens which pecked around outside the building. Once there was a rumor that sea gulls were served sometimes instead of chicken, but the biscuits and gravy were delicious anyway.

Some workers slept in their cars, shaved in the locker rooms at the plant, and ate in the mess hall. They were working seven days a week and didn't seem to be bothered by the routine.

Planks were laid so the workers could get to the commissary when it rained and not sink down to their knees in mud.

PLANT A IN 1940—This is the way it was in 1940 as Dow Plant A began to rise out of the saltgrass. Barracks and mess hall are in foreground, V-shaped office building is left of center.

IVAN ODEN—He thought he'd been sent to the end of the earth when he became the first Dow executive to stay and set up an office in Freeport in 1940 as plant construction began. He remained with the Texas Division Accounting for many years, retiring several years before his death last year.

JOHN STARK—He recalls the hectic days of 1940 when he was with Dow's Texas Division Construction Purchasing Department which was handling huge quantities of materials for building the new plant. Stark is now retired and lives at Lake Jackson Farms.

4

Dow's Coming
Boosted Economy

E. M. HENDERSON, who was with the Freeport Sulphur Company, said Dow Chemical Co. was well received by everyone when it came to Brazosport in 1940 to build the Texas Division. The merchants welcomed new business, he said, and those out of work welcomed jobs. Householders could rent any room they had to the new workers. A man on Fourth Street in Freeport even sold his chickens and converted his chicken house into a rooming house.

C. W. Vetterling of Dow's Construction Auditing Department, was lucky and got a room and bath for $30 a month, including laundry. He had been staying at the Tarpon Inn for $5 a day, which was too rich for him. He was working at the plant from "can to can't," seven days a week (80¢ an hour with overtime over 40 hours).

When Dow first came, Freeport even had a motorcycle cop.

A real frontier-type town grew up at Midway, halfway between Velasco (now Freeport north of the river) and Dow Plant A, on the shell road connecting the two.

Some little shotgun houses were converted into hotel-type buildings with cots for sleeping. The cot cost $1.50 for eight hours, then the first user got up to go to work and another warm body hit the cot for another $1.50.

There were beer joints, stores, a gas station, and even a dance hall with girls to dance with. The place was pretty wide open. Music went on in the dance hall around the clock. Nickelodeons were used most of the time, but some nights string bands were there. On weekends, even full-size dance bands of the '40s era played.

At quitting time in the afternoon, the construction workers would come out of Plant A in a line three cars wide on the old shell road, which was supposed to be only one lane each way. If the ditches were dry, the cars would come out of the plant four wide. Should you be trying to go to Plant A at the time, forget it. You really had to be on your toes not to get hit head-on.

Spring and summer of 1940 was good construction weather, but in the fall of 1940 came the rains! Contractors had never run

MIDWAY DANCE HALL—The feet that tramped through lots of mud as early Dow construction took place turned to dancing on Friday nights in this frame building at Midway, half way between Freeport and Plant A.

into such rains and mud in other parts of the country where Dow had built plants. The roads were terrible, and there were site problems for three months.

A 40 ft. by 40 ft. high tank at the plant, built on a ring foundation, settled and started to fall over. Dow then decided to skid all tanks off the foundations and drive pilings under them.

Burt Haas says the rain in 1940 caused the railroad tracks to settle into the mud and the railroad cars to tip over. Ivan Oden told of the problems of levees around the plant and no pumps to remove the rain water.

One of these times a crane got stuck in the mud, so a tractor was brought in to drag the crane out. The tractor also got stuck and another crane was brought in to get them both out. It got stuck, and still another tractor was brought in. It, too, got stuck. The two cranes and the tractors stayed there until it finally dried out.

The mud was so bad they would lose pieces of fabricated pipe and simply could not find them in the mud. The pieces of pipe had to be refabricated.

The rainy season caused the Brazos River to rise rapidly. It rose so fast one night they moved seven or eight drag lines from Plant A to the end of the waste water canal, some six or seven miles away, and put them to work. The drag lines passed dirt from one to the other and built a dam at the Brazos River where the waste water canal entered. One drag line was left in the dam with sandbags all around it.

However, life went on in Freeport. Bob Metcalf, of Dow's Marine Department, tells of a big tent west of the Tarpon Inn where there was a dance marathon going on 24 hours a day with lots of people watching. They would wear out one crew of dancers, award the prize, get some new contestants, and start again.

In the fall of 1940, there was some excitement of a different sort. An enormous whale was stranded on Surfside Beach and died there. Thousands of people came to see it.

Dow's Power I and Chlorine I plants began operating in 1940, while the magnesium plant continued under construction until 1941.

THIRD MAN—Bob Metcalf came down to Texas from Midland, Mich., with two friends. Bob was the third person hired by Dow in Texas and he went to work on April 15, 1940. His father, George Metcalf, was a longtime salesman for Dow in Midland. Bob now works in the Texas Division Marine Dept.

A WHALE OF A CROWD—It was an exciting day at Brazosport when a big whale washed ashore back in the '40s when Dow Chemical was building its first plant.

5

Thirst Dry County's Number One Ailment

BRAZORIA WAS a dry county with only beer allowed back when Dow began constructing its first facilities in the early '40s. However, ways were found to keep from being too thirsty.

You could go to Houston or across the county line in other directions, but in order to get a fifth of bourbon, we usually had to buy a case of rum. Remember the song "Rum and Coca Cola?" We brought the liquor home in the back seat under some groceries.

For nearly a year though, there was one salvation. A doctor in the area prescribed a lot of liquor for sick people. The liquor could be bought at the drugstore downstairs from his office.

One would finish work at the plant and get in line to pick up his paycheck. Then many would rush to the drugstore to get in line to see the doctor. Although the line was a couple of blocks long, it moved at a steady walk.

The doctor kept long office hours, and he knew you were ill because he had a stack of prescriptions already filled out. The prescription cost a dollar and called for either a large bottle or a small bottle, depending on how sick you were.

Then you would take the prescription down another set of

stairs which came out right in front of a cage in the pharmaceutical department. If your prescription called for a small bottle, you got a pint, which cost $5; if a large bottle, you got a quart, which cost $10.

You could call out the brand you wanted and pick it up. Most of it was whiskey, like "P. M." (for pleasant moments), or Four Roses. There was no prescription label on the bottle.

One could not sign his name to the register twice on the same day, because that was illegal. So on Saturday, in order to get some medicine to last over Sunday when the place was closed, you either had to get back in line and sign another name, or get a friend to pick up your second bottle.

This apparently legal operation lasted for less than a year. One night, unexpectedly, the whole setup just closed down forever.

JANUARY 21, 1941—DOW'S BIG DAY

January 21, 1941, was the big day for Dow Chemical's Texas Division. Even Willard Dow, president of the company, came down from Michigan for the occasion.

A row of magnesium pots was filled with cell feed, then the feed was heated with gas-fired burners to about 1,400 degrees Fahrenheit. Finally, the electric current was turned on to the cell feed and molten magnesium metal began to come to the top. Clarence Hock, employee with the longest service in the Midland, Michigan Magnesium Department, dipped and poured the first metal.

About 20 pounds of magnesium was dipped off and put into molds for souvenirs. Then the other cells were dipped and the plant was in operation, extracting magnesium metal from the sea.

The original 12 million pounds per year magnesium plant was increased to 18 million pounds when the British Government, in the fall of 1940, contracted for a six-million-pounds per year addition to the original plant.

After the plant start up, there followed a number of weeks of problems with low cell efficiency because of the presence of boron. This problem was solved by March.

The first shipment of magnesium to a customer was in early February, 1941, when a truckload of ingots was loaded and shipped to Reynolds Metals Co. at Lister Hill, Alabama.

FIRST METAL—Dr. A. P. Beutel, center front, first general manager of the Texas Division. This picture was taken at the first anniversary of making magnesium from the sea.

WORKERS RAN FROM HURRICANE

Hurricanes were a threat from time to time. During the first hurricane in 1941, the Dow people left hurriedly, while the Freeport Sulphur Company people didn't seem worried. As the Dow people drove out Second Street ahead of the storm, they looked in the window of the McFarland home, where the manager of the Sulphur Company plant lived, and saw people quietly playing bridge.

One longtime Freeport resident told some Dow people, "Don't worry, the Coast Guard is standing by." When the Dow folks returned after the storm, the Coast Guard boat was stranded on top of a levee and didn't get back into the water for several months.

"DON'T WORRY"—When the first hurricane threat came, the newly-arrived Dow people were told not to worry—"The Coast Guard is standing by." But when the evacuees returned they found even the CG boat stranded atop a levee!

6

Area Blacked Out; Beefed Up Guard

AL DEERE tells of arriving in Freeport in 1941, and starting to work as head of security for Dow. There was a mounted patrol already established with eight horses. Besides patrolling, the mounted men carried messages back and forth where cars couldn't go. Automotive vehicles were in short supply and in poor shape. A two-wheeled, horse-drawn sulky was even used for a time.

After Pearl Harbor and the declaration of war, the FBI, under executive order, picked up and put into protective custody several people in Velasco and Midway who had been under suspicion as enemy supporters. One had in his back room an enlargement of Hitler's picture and a swastica. However, after interrogation, they were all released without any derogatory record.

On the afternoon of Pearl Harbor, December 7, 1941, the National Guard was called on for help. At 7 p.m. the next day, the now famous 36th Division arrived. It had been inducted into the regular army. They set up ground stations at critical locations in the area.

The 36th Division left in a year or so and next showed up in

33

Italy at Salerno, where those who survived became heroes.

There were 250 Military Police stationed here. Also, two companies of infantry were emplaced to secure the harbor. The Coast Guard beefed up its operations with 80 horse-mounted policemen, and Doberman Pinscher dogs to sniff out landing parties along the coast.

Some of the military were placed in quarters in Freeport on West Second Street. Temporary buildings, a recreation hall, etc., were put up and everything was kept clean and orderly.

Freeport girls would come out to USO parties in the recreation hall.

At one time, there were also eight anti-aircraft detachments around the Dow plant. The coast was patrolled by two or three dirigibles stationed at Hitchcock, and by PBY flying boats.

During wartime, a blackout directive was received. Many lights were put out, but the rest were hooded so they could not be

COFFEE BREAK—Dow's first general manager, Dr. A. P. Beutel, left, takes a coffee break with J. P. Bryan, a Freeport attorney who was hired by Dow as the Texas Division counsel. It is from his family that the name of Bryan Beach is derived.

seen from above. Also, street lights were turned off, black shades were put in windows, and hoods were put on automobile lights.

After the blackout was in effect, you could drive into the area from Angleton at night and only a few little lights could be seen here and there. It looked as if these were lights from a few farm houses and not a big chemical company.

During wartime, identification badges were a "must," and the security people were very strict. One time, Dr. A. P. Beutel, the Dow general manager, tried to get into Ethyl Dow without his pass. When he was stopped, he said, "I am A. P. Beutel, the plant manager of the Texas Division." The security man answered, "I don't care if you're the Pope, you don't come in here without a badge."

In the early '40s in Brazosport, as the Dow Chemical plants were taking shape in the salt grass, beer was scarce. The beer joints would open each day, one by one. The first one would open at 7 a.m. and close at 9 a.m. The place could sell its whole stock in about two hours.

People would bring gallon jugs, buckets, and other containers to get draft beer. The bottle beer would be from other states and people in Texas were not familiar with it. The draft beer, of course, could be any brand.

Some would bring a gallon pickle jar and a loaf of bread to get the tap beer. When the jar was filled, a slice of bread was put over

AL DEERE—Al Deere, who had worked for the Federal Bureau of Investigation, came in 1941 to Freeport to head up Dow's Texas Division security department. Now retired, Deere and his wife live at Lake Jackson Farms.

the top and the lid screwed down. The yeast and salt in the bread somehow kept the beer from going flat until they got home. After arriving home, the bread was spooned out of the beer and it was ready to drink.

In about two hours, after the first place sold out, the proprietor told which joint would be open next. Then all the cars would take off in a caravan to the next place. It looked like the plant was letting out.

The people would go to the Brown Room, Tumble Inn, Jimmy's Cafe, Bearhunter's Cafe, Barney Dunn's, The Oasis, and others. About 150 cars would start out in the morning, and by the time they made the last stop, the line was down to about 20 cars.

7

Bridge Jams;
Road Built Overnight

HARLAND SHERBROOK told a good story about the early days when Dow Chemical Co. first came to this area. The only road from Freeport to the plant site in the early days was across the railroad bridge, which was also a turn-bridge for barges. One night a boat got stuck in the opening, and the bridge could not be re-turned to connect the road.

When A. P. Beutel found out about it, he knew no one could get from Freeport to the plant the next morning. He called Sherbrook and told him to build a road across the dam at the end of the harbor that night. Sherbrook got the men and the equipment going and the road was ready by morning.

*

Those were busy days and lots of us worked all day and into the night, including Saturdays and many Sundays. Once in a while when we got an evening off, we would sometimes drive over to Pearson's, a delightful restaurant on the San Bernard, run by Ebbie and Eva Pearson.

At Pearson's there was a gal none of us will ever forget—Viola

37

Guthrie. She was tall and lean, and wore her hair coiled on her head in the shape of a coronet. Viola was queen of the establishment—head waitress, maitre d', specialty cook, and your friend and mine if she liked you. If the table ordered a round of beer, she wrapped a towel around a dozen bottles and brought them to the table on her hip, where she snapped the caps off one by one.

In those days, there were few good places to eat in the Freeport area, so when we had the chance, we went to Pearson's. They served delicious fried chicken, special slaw, dreamy french fries, and great homemade biscuits with cream gravy. If Ebbie could get good steaks that day, you might order a steak instead of chicken. If the steaks didn't meet his rigid requirements, he didn't buy any that day and they were off the menu.

As you can imagine, the place was crowded with hungry folks, but Viola kept everyone in order. She had a ball bat nearby and didn't mind brandishing the bat when needed.

*

I must tell you something of the Freeport Sulphur Company hotel, the Tarpon Inn, which was located where Intermedics now is in downtown Freeport. This was headquarters for Dow people in 1939 and 1940, and was a community landmark here until 1954. The Inn, which was finished a short time before Freeport was founded in 1912, resembled an English tavern put down on the salt grass prairie. Texas newspapers hailed it as an "outstanding hotel on the Texas plains."

The exterior was of cream-colored stucco, trimmed in dark brown wood. The distinguished architecture was said to be a mixture of Tudor and Mission styles. Many of the 30 guest rooms had fireplaces and private baths. All had high ceilings. There was a public bath on each floor, several plush guest parlors, a large dining room, and a well-designed kitchen.

When Dow first came to Freeport, E. D. "Spot," Brockman was the manager. His was an illustrious career as hotel manager, entertainment and party impresario, civic leader, and special ambassador of the Sulphur Company to the area.

Reese Austin came to the Inn with "Spot." Reese was bellhop,

TARPON INN—The downtown Freeport area now occupied by Intermedics was once the site of this picturesque inn. As seen in March 1940, the Tarpon Inn was headquarters for both Dow and the Austin Company which was building the Dow plants.

bell captain, waiter, master bartender, relief desk clerk, and just general handyman.

Poker was one of the recreational activities that went on after dinner on Saturday evening. I remember a few of these occasions. Parlor 14 was the location. The games would go on till late at night. Then "Spot", with his ready helper, Reese, would whip up a midnight breakfast of ham, eggs, sausage, hot cakes, toast and coffee for the weary players.

Many of the Dow folks shed a tear when the times changed and in 1954 the hotel was torn down.

*

When my family came to Freeport, we stayed at the new Dow Hotel (now the Freeport Inn) for six weeks. My wife knew she

SPOT BROCKMAN— The late E. D. "Spot" Brockman was not a Dow man but he was indeed closely involved with the Dow operations in the early days. He helped provide food and entertainment for hundreds of Dow people.

would have time on her hands, so she brought along her sewing machine in the car from Michigan. She did more sewing at the hotel than before or since. Our daughter was the only child staying at the hotel, and her pastime was to visit the other Dow wives staying there.

The hotel did not have a dining room at that time, so we had many meals at the Sweet Shop, a cafe on Park Avenue. Their delicious homemade pies helped me put on 10 pounds I really didn't need.

8

Shift Workers Shared Same Bed

I NEED to mention another boarding house which was well-known when Dow Chemical Co. first came to Freeport. It was Emma Adams' place on Fifth Street (she later moved to a larger place on Fourth Street).

In 1940 when Dow came, construction workers slept in cars, chicken houses, cow barns—anywhere. The few cafes were so crowded, many men went to work without breakfast or lunch.

The working men were in need of some place to get away from the mosquitoes, so being both kindhearted and depression poor, Emma started a rooming house and dining room. She had three bedrooms and a large screened porch which was also used as a bedroom. She rented three of the rooms to 14 men who slept in shifts. While one shift worked, another shift slept. Room and board was $10 a week.

She fed the 14 men, and others, too, in the large dining room. They sat at a long homemade table, with as many as 40 to 60 a day eating in shifts.

Emma would get up at 2:30 a.m. to start breakfast and make lunches. The men had to be at Dow by 7 a.m. Since it took about an hour to get there because of the bad roads and heavy traffic, breakfast was on the table by 4:30 a.m. She also served noon dinner and a night meal, plus lots of sandwiches for men on the night shift.

Some people slept on the living room floor to keep out of the mosquitoes. They were mostly older men; the younger men had gone to war. It was almost impossible to rent apartments, so the workers would leave their families at home and come here to work.

Once in a while a kook would show up. One said the coffee was so hot he couldn't drink it. The maid told him it would cost 25¢ to cool it.

*

In March of 1941, Ethyl Dow produced the first bromine. Work also started on a new $8 million addition to the magnesium plant, financed by a federal grant. It was labeled Defense Plant Corporation Job No. 81.

In July, 1941, there was a bad fire in the power house. It was a serious fire and the first big one in the Dow Texas Division. It caused a shutdown of the chemical plants. Sabotage was suspected, but after the whole area was carefully inspected, no evidence of sabotage was found.

Nig Raney tells how in 1941 lots of shrimp and crabs were taken from the seawater intake and those nearby had a free lunch. The lunch period was one hour then, and with a little fire the seafood was cooked and eaten.

Raney says that in the summer, high school students were hired to work in the plant. One of the kids asked him if Ethyl Dow (a plant) was Dr. Willard Dow's daughter.

In the beginning of the Texas Division, only single women could be hired. If one married, she had to leave in six months. Mabel Helen Stratton was the first to stay after she married I. E. Warren. After Pearl Harbor, married women were needed, so they were hired and continued to work.

Women were not allowed to smoke at their desks, and they could not wear slacks to work. Dow finally found that too much time was being wasted smoking in the lounges, so women were allowed to smoke at their desks.

The Alden Dow houses, completed in Freeport in the summer of 1941, were quite controversial. They had central heating and were on a concrete slab. He had them painted in California colors of orange and apple green.

The Showboat Theater in Freeport put on real live vaudeville acts between shows. "Judge" Brock, later a Justice of the Peace, was accompanist for the live shows.

The hoosegow in Freeport was a bleak concrete block building with no heat. The prisoners wanted blankets to keep them warm, but the mayor said no. He didn't want them to be too comfortable there.

BOARDING HOUSE—Emma Adams operated a popular boarding house in Freeport in the '40s. She stopped serving meals in the '70s, but continued to take in roomers until recently when she retired after 41 years of service.

ALDEN DOW—The architect brother of Willard Dow, who was then company president, designed the houses above, that Dow built in Freeport in 1941. He also laid out the Lake Jackson townsite.

9

Hurricane Warning Caused Concern

MANY OF us came down from Michigan to help build the Freeport plants. We'd never had hurricanes in Michigan and, of course, we were worried about the terrible hurricanes people told about on the Gulf Coast.

The 1900 hurricane in Galveston, and the 1932 hurricane in Brazoria County, were the subjects of tales of terror told by the natives who had lived through them. So, when the first hurricane warning came in 1941, we were more than a little concerned.

It was on a Sunday. The weather was sunny and beautiful. After church in the morning, we went home to dinner and then to a show at the Ora Theater on Park Avenue in the afternoon. When we came out of the show, the weather was still beautiful, but there were hurricane warning flags flying at the foot of Park Avenue. We went on home and still the weather looked good.

The next morning, as many of the wives did their laundry and hung the clothes on the line, the wind started blowing hard and it began raining. That's all we needed to call the Rice Hotel in Houston for a room reservation, and then drive up there for refuge.

45

When we arrived at the Rice, it seemed that half of Freeport was there, and hurricane parties were already underway. We weathered the storm there comfortably and safely, and returned home in a couple of days to find lots of water in the streets. We now considered ourselves hurricane veterans.

The Dow plant shut down for the hurricane from September 18 through September 24. It came through the storm with only minor damage, a tribute to the careful design and engineering by George Greene, chief engineer, and his crew.

*

In 1941, the Dow Texas Division commenced the production of magnesium, caustic soda, ethylene, ethylene dichloride, ethylene glycol and propylene dichloride.

The Dow and British Government's first plants had been in production several months, and the Defense Plant Corporation Project No. 81 was to be completed in November of 1941. These, together, would have a capacity of 36 million pounds of magnesium per year.

In June of 1941, the Office of Production Management in Washington announced that Dow's magnesium plant in Freeport would be doubled again—to be finished in 1942. Austin Company engineers set up in the M and M Building in Houston to work on the design of the new plant. It was to be designed for 72 million pounds per year of magnesium.

The new plant site would be on a 670-acre tract west of Velasco, west of the waste water canal, and south of the projected new Highway 288. The site was in the middle of a lot of five-acre tracts, and was to be condemned by the government if it could not be bought at a reasonable price.

A new subsidiary, called "Dow Magnesium Corporation," was formed to build the new government-owned, Dow-operated magnesium plant. Dow called the job "Dow Magnesium Plant B."

The schedule for completion was 12 months. Harland Sherbrook told of the hurry-up schedule to build Dow Magnesium Plant B.

Texas Division General Manager, Dr. A. P. Beutel, was always known for short production schedules, which made it

FLOODED—Freeport streets were flooded after the 1941 hurricane, the first encountered by the Dow people.

difficult to figure a practical schedule for this job. The War Production Board was putting on heavy pressure. Beutel's original estimate of two years had been revised to a year and a half, but the War Department said it would have to be built in less than a year.

The drawback was having only one railroad and an old oyster shell road into the plant site—the old Tater Jones Road. It looked like it simply wouldn't be possible to bring in the materials as fast as they would be needed.

Again Sherbrook figured as tightly as possible. He wanted 10 months, but Beutel told him to do it in eight.

Two weeks after Pearl Harbor Day, in December, 1941, Sam Anderson, of the War Production Board, met here with Beutel, Sherbrook, and George McGranahan, demanding the schedule be cut to six months. It really looked impossible.

Between December 17, when we got the word to go ahead, and the first of January, we were getting into motion. We actually got underway on January 1, and made magnesium on June 26—less than six months. This construction miracle required innovative ways of doing things, and I will tell about them in several later columns.

EQUINE STAR—The late George McGranahan posed in front of his ranch house at Lake Jackson on Anaconcho Rebel who was ridden by Leslie Howard in "Gone With the Wind." Alden Dow owned the horse and occasionally went to the ranch to ride him. McGranahan was Dow assistant general manager in charge of engineering and construction.

10

*Dr. Beutel Good
At Picking People*

BEFORE WE begin to watch the construction of Dow Magnesium Plant B, with all the wartime problems and obstructions which were so brilliantly overcome by Dow, I would like to tell you about a dynamic figure in the development and growth of Dow's Texas Division—A. P. Beutel. He received an honorary doctorate of engineering in 1942 from his alma mater, Case Institute of Technology in Cleveland. Thus, many knew him only as Dr. Beutel. When I went to work for him in 1937, he was just known as A. P. Beutel or "Dutch" Beutel.

At that time, he was the one and only assistant general manager of the whole Dow Chemical Co. He reported to General Manager, Willard Dow, son of the founder, H. H. Dow. Willard Dow also had two other titles—that of president of the company and chairman of the board.

A. P. Beutel had a degree in mining and metallurgical engineering from Case, and joined Dow in 1916 as an engineering draftsman. He worked his way up to assistant general manager of Dow by 1932. He was also treasurer, and later, president of Dowell, the oil service company.

I was lucky enough to be asked to join him, along with

Charlie Penhaligen and Russ Crawford of Dowell, when they made the 1937 trip around the United States to inspect Dowell operations. While on this trip, Beutel noted the flaring of waste natural gas in the Southwest, which started him thinking about using that gas to produce chemicals. This was one of the reasons why Dow started the Texas Division in 1940.

I have told you a little about Dow coming to Freeport in 1939 and 1940. To set the stage for Dow's enormously successful growth, however, you need to know more about A. P. Beutel.

One of his characteristics was the ability to pick young people and groom them for top management and technical jobs at Dow. He often gave credit to the remarkable ability and drive of some top people he brought with him from Michigan.

These included men like George McGranahan, assistant general manager in charge of engineering and construction of Dow Magnesium Plant B; George Greene, chief engineer; Harland Sherbrook, construction and maintenance manager; C. M. Shigley, plant manager of Dow Magnesium Plant B; Ivan Oden, chief auditor; Dave Landsborough, comptroller; and, N. D. Griswold, manager of power, and later, of engineering. There were many others, too, picked by Beutel who made important contributions to the Texas Division of Dow.

I had the privilege of being Beutel's private secretary from 1937 to the 1940s. I was then given other duties, but still reported directly to him.

Many memories of the '40s, and some even later, come back now:

—Bootjacks in Beutel's executive office to pull off the mud-covered boots used to tramp over the new construction site.

—The free-form table used by Beutel for his operating board meetings, designed so he could look every one of his assistants right in the eye. (It's now in the conference room at the Brazosport Center for the Arts and Sciences).

—The day when he walked down the hall in A-1201 to use the men's room. He opened the door, saw four stalls and four pairs of feet protruding from the stalls. So he shut the door, walked back to his office and called Pete Peterson, the carpenter superintendent, to come in.

Beutel took Pete by the arm and walked him to one corner of

DYNAMIC LEADER—Dr. A. P. "Dutch" Beutel was the first general manager of Dow's Texas Division, watching it constructed from the ground up and continuing to head its progress for many years afterward. His influence is still felt in the company worldwide through the young men he selected and groomed in the Texas Division. Many of them rose to take top Dow management positions both here and abroad in numerous divisions of the chemical company.

---

the office where Beutel leaned down to the floor and drew a circle with a piece of chalk. Beutel said, "Pete, tomorrow morning I am going to come to this spot and use a new commode you are going to install tonight." Pete was ready for him the next morning.

—The time in winter when a strike was in progress. It was cold and raining. Beutel ordered some rubber slickers for the strikers on the picket line and some scrap lumber so they could build a fire to keep warm. One of the supervisors asked Beutel what he was doing that for. He answered, "Those fellows were my men before they went on strike, and they'll be my men when it is over." The slickers and the wood were delivered as ordered.

Beutel had a unique ability to look forward many years and plan for the Texas Division. I remember when the federal government wanted Dow to double the magnesium capacity. They wanted him to build the addition alongside of Plant A, but Beutel steadfastly refused, saying the government should provide a site farther away, where Plant B is now located. A lot of pressure was put up by the feds, but eventually they agreed to Beutel's plan.

The point was that the property for Plant B was divided up into a myriad of five-acre tracts with ownership scattered and lost. Dow could never have negotiated the purchase in years. The federal government took them all over in a few weeks (with payment in escrow for the owners who could not be found) and established good title to the property. After World War II, when the government sold the property, Dow was able to purchase it with good title because Beutel had had the vision to look far ahead.

Beutel also taught me the value of quality. When I was in charge of the Dow Hotel and we were going to purchase furniture for a new addition, I recommended we buy chairs with narrow arm rests so no one could leave a cigarette on the arm and cause a burn. Beutel told me he was tired of those sharp uncomfortable chair arms, which he detested whenever he traveled. He said our hotel would have comfortable arm rests wide enough to rest the body of the weary traveler. We bought the comfortable chairs.

He also taught me the value of good food properly prepared. We bought the best food and meats for our hotel, cafeterias, and hospital, and hired cooks who could prepare it right. Later, when we added the fishing reservoirs and Dow Lodge as part of our operations, it was Dr. and Mrs. Beutel who trained the cooks to prepare and serve the finest meals one could find outside of the big city clubs.

Lastly, I remember Beutel as being a stickler for promptness.

When we were running the Dow airport, and had planes flying to Michigan nearly every day, Dr. Beutel traveled a lot, and he set the departure time for his flights.

When he told the other passengers to be at the Dow airport for a 7:30 a.m. departure, he meant that at promptly 7:30 the Dow plane would be speeding down the runway and the wheels would be pulling up into the fuselage as the minute hand passed over the 7:30 mark. A few passengers who drove up to the airport at 7:30 could only wave goodbye to the plane.

Beutel is a person for whom a whole book should be written, and I will mention him many times again in my future Episodes. At the testimonial dinner honoring Beutel's 50 years with Dow, which was held at the Warwick Hotel in Houston on November 1, 1966, it was said:

> *"He is a man of boundless energy and drive, a man of ideas and imagination. He is, at the same time, practical, perservering and proud. But, most of all, Dutch Beutel is the pioneering personality of the chemical industry in the Southwest."*

11

Dow Used Innovative Delivery Means

DOW MAGNESIUM Plant B was indeed a construction miracle. To go from raw prairie land to a working 72-million-pound per year magnesium plant in less than six months is hard to believe unless you were here to see it happen. To accomplish this feat in such a short time meant new ways of doing things.

For an example, let's look at purchasing. John Stark was supervisor of purchasing for the Dow Mag Plant B job. He had 65 men, located all over the United States, acting for him to contact the vendors and then follow through on the shipments.

The short construction schedule meant everything must come into Velasco (the section of Freeport north of the river) on an exact date. For instance, just the materials needed for 12,000 workmen at the plant included three million drinking cups, $10,000 worth of boots, $20,000 worth of paint brushes, $1,000 worth of pencils, etc.

Stark's men worked out of New York, Cleveland, Chicago, Philadelphia and Los Angeles. He used a local Dow office and a Dow man at each location for contact with his field men. An example of the tight scheduling was the delivery of components for the cell feed operation.

Say this is Wednesday morning. Stark calls his man in Milwaukee and tells him to pick up a Faulk reducer from the manufacturer in Milwaukee and put it on a baggage car connected to a passenger train in Milwaukee. The man then gets on the baggage car—not a passenger car—and watches the reducer all the way to Chicago, where another passenger train is waiting on the track for the Milwaukee train.

In Chicago, the man sees that the reducer is put on the station cart and taken to the other train where it is put on the baggage car headed for Houston. The train arrives in Houston about noon on Thursday where Stark has a truck meet the passenger train and take the reducer to the plant in Velasco.

At the same time on Wednesday, another man in Ohio picks up an elevator chain at the manufacturer and puts it on a baggage car headed for St. Louis. He rides the baggage car with it to St. Louis and sees it is transferred to the Sunshine Special which arrives in Houston about noon on Thursday. The same truck picks up the chain in Houston and takes it to the Velasco plant for installation that afternoon.

This means that a reducer in Milwaukee on Wednesday, and an elevator chain in Ohio on Wednesday, are brought together at the plant and installed to start working Thursday night.

Another example was a freight gondola loaded with cable coming into Houston on the Sunshine Special passenger train. The gondola was positioned ahead of the locomotive on the train.

Still another example—we needed extremely long power poles. Stark's man found the poles in East Texas, but there was no way to get them out to the railroad because of rain and mud. Stark's man found a farmer, rented horses and dragged the poles out of the woods to the railroad.

They had to buy a lot of used equipment to get it quick. Used pumps were bought from gravel pits in Michigan, from mines in Colorado, from a copper mine in Arizona, and a salvage yard in San Francisco.

*

Meanwhile on Monday p.m., March 16, 1942, it was raining in torrents. There were no paved highways, and nearby was Dow

Mag Plant B coming up out of the mud. Up till then, there was no place to spot trailers near the plant, and now a new trailer park was about to open. It had four large service buildings with laundry equipment, showers and lavatories. More than 100 trailers filled with people were lined up for hours waiting in the rain.

Jack Crockett, the manager, gave the signal, and the trailers moved in. Twenty men worked all afternoon and all night spotting trailers. In 24 hours, the park was filled to capacity with 128 trailers. Work went on to double the capacity to an additional 128 trailers 10 days later. Soon, across the road from the private trailer park, a new park was opened with 400 government-owned trailers to rent.

A Spears Dairy Store (something like the 7-11 stores we are familiar with) opened in the park, and this was followed by a post office substation, a nursery school to care for 100 children,

KIDDIE CARE—
Children of war workers connected with the Dow plant construction were cared for in a $30,000 federal government project called the Trailer Park Child Care Center. It was operated through the Velasco Independent School District, later consolidated into the present Brazosport district. Here, some of the pre-school children are eating their noon meal. Louise King was supervisor and Pat C. Caruthers, superintendent.

and a small community center.

Monroe Schrader, then with Dow Payroll Department, tells of living in the trailer park. On a Sunday afternoon, they would set up chairs outdoors on the shell and visit with their neighbors while enjoying a cool refreshing drink.

TRAILER PARK—Many people helping bring the early Dow plants out of the mud and into wartime production maintained their first Brazosport homes here.

JACK CROCKETT—Managing the trailer park for Dow back in the early '40s was Jack Crockett. He is now a Houston resident.

12

Big Canal—Another Quick Job

PART OF the construction of Plant B was the building of a huge barge canal running some seven miles from the Gulf of Mexico up to the Plant B site. Harland Sherbrook again told about this gigantic project.

Plant B was different from Plant A. Plant A was close to the intake for seawater, and waste water was dumped into the river seven miles away. Plant B was close to the discharge canal, but the seawater had to be brought seven miles. Also, in order to get barge shipments of shell, there had to be a barge canal.

The canal served several purposes. Seawater for cooling water. . .seawater for the Mag Plant. . .and a barge canal to float shell up to the plant. It was a tremendous project—a canal nearly seven miles long with 3,200,000 yards of dirt to remove.

Bids were requested several ways, for dredging with different size dredges or draglines. Also, bids were asked to include large Monagan rigs from the Mississippi River levees. Surprisingly enough, when bids were received, the large Monagan draglines came in with prices Dow could hardly believe.

The bid price per yard was one-third of all other bids; actually 9.7¢ per cubic yard. Even at that price, the contractor made so much money, the government made him renegotiate the contract and he had to return some of the money to the government.

Sherbrook talked to the Atlas Construction Co. representatives. They said they would move in three large, seven- or eight-yard bucket rigs with 175-ft. booms. He couldn't believe they could handle that much dirt. Atlas said they would use the rigs around the clock, seven days a week.

That night when Sherbrook got home, he knew the canal would have to be finished in four months. So he knew how much they would have to move an hour.

The next morning, he asked the Atlas man what he would figure they could move per hour, planning for seven days a week, 24 hours a day, and necessary downtime. Atlas said they would guarantee 500 yards per machine or 1,500 yards per hour for three rigs.

They had hit the nail right on the head as Sherbrook had

REMINISCING—Bertha Spencer reminisces over an old copy of a menu from the Port Cafe which became a Freeport landmark and the setting of many a memorable breakfast.

WHAT A DRAG!—A Monagan dragline begins work on Dow's big barge canal. The project was completed in less than five months.

---

figured. They moved in the middle of January and started a few days later.

Atlas had some problems with unions until the unions found they didn't have anyone who knew how to operate the rigs.

In addition to digging the canal and leveling off the sides for levees, there were three big road bridges and a railroad bridge to build.

Atlas moved on the job in the middle of January, and water was turned into the canal about June 12—a little over four and one-half months later.

*

Meanwhile, I must tell you of a cafe in Freeport called the Port Cafe. It was run by brothers Bob and Jack Spencer. They were ably assisted by Bob's wife, Cora, and Jack's wife, Bertha.

The Port Cafe opened in June of 1929 in downtown Freeport. As business grew, their cafe was enlarged several times. Their claim to fame at the time was their famous breakfast for parties of deep sea fishermen and for duck hunters during hunting

61

season. I even enjoyed a couple of these trips myself.

The deep sea fishing parties would meet about 2 a.m. at this cafe for breakfast before starting out on a fishing jaunt which would last all day. Fishermen came from as far as Dallas, El Paso, and places in Oklahoma to fish in these parties.

For breakfast there was the usual bacon and eggs, hot cakes and homemade sausage, country pork chops, and something we don't see around here anymore, country ham and red eye gravy. The fishermen would be served and out by 3 or 3:30 a.m. and carry a lunch on the boat. They would return to dock late in the afternoon.

Shrimp and oysters abounded in the nearby Gulf waters, so the cafe had lots of fresh oysters for stew, fried oysters and cocktails. The Port Cafe was known as the best place for oysters anywhere around.

The restaurant was sold in 1968, but this was a landmark restaurant for many, many years in Freeport.

13

Camp Chemical Houses
Went Up Quickly

ON JANUARY 27, 1942, the *Velasco World* Extra Edition announced a $3,250,000 housing program for Velasco, work to start at once. This would include 3,000 houses, 44 barracks, 45 utility buildings, a mess hall to seat 1,000, commissaries, a bank, stores, a post office, and a fire department. The program was to provide temporary housing for the thousands of workers building the new 72-million-pound per year magnesium plant.

The houses would be 16 ft. by 16 ft., composed of two bedrooms, a living room, a two-burner hotplate with a portable oven, and a sink. They would rent for $10 a week, with water, gas and lights furnished.

Forty-five utility buildings, 24 ft. by 56 ft., containing baths, lavatories, toilets, and laundry facilities, were to be constructed for the occupants of the 3,000 houses.

In addition, there would be 44 barracks, 24 ft. by 216 ft., to house 120 men each. A huge mess hall, which would accommodate 1,000 men, would also be constructed.

The *Velasco World* said, "Contrary to popular belief, and a shock to the business interests of both Velasco and Freeport, comes the announcement that stores, commissaries, a post office, a bank, and a fire department will be provided on land just west of the proposed magnesium plant." Alden Dow was the architect for the huge housing project, and the entire operation was to be about three miles from Velasco.

On February 21, 1942, the first construction shack was put up at Camp Chemical. On Sunday, March 29, the Camp Chemical Cafeteria (1,050 seating) served its first meal. It would thereafter be open 24 hours a day.

On Saturday, April 23, Camp Chemical was formally opened for inspection. The housing project to care for 10,000 defense workers had been built in a little more than six weeks.

All this wasn't easy, either. Heavy rains held up the work for days. Plank roads were laid over the slushy quagmire so materials could be trucked into the sites. The prairie flooded so deeply that the wooden pavements floated around.

The little houses were planted on small concrete foundations 14 feet apart in rows, with 30 feet between the rows. A lavatory and shower room served every 14 houses, and for every 100, there was a laundry building.

There were no garages, and tenants had to bring their own furniture. The only telephones at Camp Chemical were in the Administration Building.

Camp Chemical was owned and operated by the Defense Plant Corporation, and it was the only enterprise of its kind in the world. It was built under the direction of C. H. Van Eman, Construction Supervisor.

When construction was finished, there were actually 45 barracks for 4,400 men and 60 women, a post office, 2,300 one-room homes for men, women and families, a general store, cafeteria, jail, fire department, clinic, recreation building, utilities, and its own water and sewer systems.

The cafeteria covered almost a block of ground. It was clean, spacious and cool.

The rates were first set at $10 a week, including utilities, for the 16 ft. by 16 ft. houses, but later they were able to reduce the rates to $7 a week for a family or for two men. Rates at the barracks were $5 a week, including linen service, both in the men's and women's barracks.

Hundreds of carloads of crushed rock were used to surface the miles of streets in Camp Chemical. Monroe Schrader, of Dow's Accounting Department, lived there for a short time and remembers how it would cut tires and was very difficult to walk on.

Ed Kilman of the *Houston Post* reported that some of the 16 ft. by 16 ft. houses were built in 10 minutes each, and not with mirrors.

The structures were prefabricated. The four walls came ready-made, complete with windows and doorway. The flat roof came in one piece, as did the pine floor. Everything was ready to assemble and nail together when the actual erection of the house began. There were three or four carpenters at each corner and two in between (more than 2,000 carpenters on the project at the same time).

To give you an idea of the carpenters' speed, "Mayor" H. J. Passmore, the project manager, recounted: "A recreation building, to be used as temporary living quarters by a detachment of soldiers, was to be completed by a certain day.

"A sergeant reported to his lieutenant on that day that it had not even been started. The officer, a little sore, went to the campsite to complain about it. By the time he got there, the building was finished."

An employee in the Camp Chemical Administration Building topped that one—"I went from my office to another office to take some papers. I stayed just long enough to go over them briefly. As I started back, I looked out and a house had been built out in front."

CIRCA 1942—The top photograph shows the shacks that existed on the river before the Camp Chemical housing program went into effect. The housing project included 3,000 houses, 44 barracks, 45 utility buildings, commissaries and mess hall to house the thousands of workers building the magnesium plant. In the bottom photograph, lines form at one of the commissaries. Construction began on the site in February of 1942 and the camp officially opened in April of that year.

14

Store & Cafeteria
Highlighted Camp Chemical

I REMEMBER well Roland Mason's big general store at Camp Chemical. It occupied most of a city block, and was the largest and most complete general store ever seen in this area. A shrewd executive, Mr. Mason used big city merchandising ideas in the successful operation of his gigantic enterprise. He not only solved the shopping problems of the thousands of construction workers living in Camp Chemical, but the residents of the surrounding area as well.

Everything from dog biscuits to living room furniture could be found in the general store. It carried groceries, meats, fresh vegetables, drugs, dry goods, work clothing, hardware, confections, and hundreds of other articles. Besides all that, the store did an extensive banking business. About a half-million dollars in construction payroll checks were cashed at the bank windows of the store every Friday. The money was brought from Houston in armored trucks, fully guarded by uniformed men with rifles.

There were refrigerator cases lining two sides of the building, which displayed fresh meats, specially-prepared meats, and dozens of kinds of fine cheeses. Fresh fruits and vegetables—the

67

ROLAND MASON'S STORE

largest assortment in these parts—were also displayed in long
refrigerated rows. Long shelves running from floor to ceiling
featured an enormous variety of canned goods.

Other sections in the store featured books and magazines, a
modern drug counter, and a furniture showroom. Prices were
competitive, too, and many housewives came from the area to
shop in the mornings when traffic was less congested.

Mason conserved tires and gas by getting around the camp
area in a covered horse-drawn surrey.

*

Here we should take a few moments to discuss the women's
barracks at Camp Chemical. Two barracks buildings, situated
by themselves, were assigned to 60 young women employed by
the war industries in the Freeport-Velasco area.

While each of the men's barracks was built to accommodate
100 to 120 men, the women's barracks provided more spacious

THE WAY IT WAS—Life in Camp Chemical in the early 1940's was quite an experience as remembered by a few former residents of the facility. The top photo is a view of the camp's barracks. Below, the large camp cafeteria served many purposes and was said to feature "excellent cuisine."

quarters for the women. There were also living rooms where the girls played bridge, read, talked and danced. A radio-phonograph combination was also included, as well as comfortable, attractive chrome furniture. The feminine touch could be seen in the women's barracks with customary lacy curtains and frills.

Mrs. Amy Hall was the hostess in charge of the women's barracks and the recreation building. The girls enjoyed complete freedom and there was no curfew.

Living was very economical. The girls paid only $4 a week for their room, so most of their money went for clothes, war bonds and miscellaneous items.

Finger Furniture Company furnished the men's and women's barracks with: 4,320 beds, 4,320 mattresses, 8,600 pillow cases, 7,200 blankets, 16,800 towels, 2,300 mirrors, 4,520 pillows, 16,800 sheets, 2,308 chests, and 3,800 chairs. They bragged that all of these items were delivered to Camp Chemical within 60 days after the order was placed.

*

Another feature of Camp Chemical that particularly appealed to me was the big cafeteria. When the 1,000-seat cafeteria was opened, "Mayor" H. J. Passmore invited the general public to come and partake of the "excellent cuisine" of W. T. Swafford who operated the cafeteria. Swafford was a graduate of the Palmer House and other notable caravansaries.

An advertisement for the cafeteria offered a "wide variety of delicious food at popular prices," and stated they catered to banquets, parties, luncheons and meetings. Their slogan was, "Largest—Best Eating Place in Brazoria County."

John Suggs, then with Dow's Engineering Department, remembers attending a big party at the cafeteria put on by the Austin Company. A dance band was on hand, and this was one of the social highlights of the time.

15

Camp Chemical Dances Were Big Events

MYRTLE CROSBY, who is now Mrs. "Speedy" Bullard of Lake Jackson, worked in the Camp Chemical post office in 1943, so she remembers the big housing project, thousands of people living there, and the mud in the streets as Dow's first plants took shape.

The post office staff, among their other duties, sold war bonds. Myrtle remembers a war bond promotion when Jennifer Jones and western film star, "Big Boy" Williams, came to the area to help sell bonds. This was a big event. The stars stayed for part of two days, and made appearances at the Freeport hotel called the Tarpon Inn, and at all the post offices, including the one at Camp Chemical.

In the post office there was a big bulletin board. Everyone put notes on the board for such things as rooms and apartments for rent, stuff to sell or exchange, etc. Myrtle remembers selling a trailer house from a bulletin board notice.

Camp Chemical had its own ball park. Myrtle was a member of a girls' softball team and played many games, including one county-wide league tournament.

The Camp Chemical cafeteria provided a place for

socializing. Meetings of women's groups were held there in the afternoon. Many people would bring their families to the cafeteria for supper and for Sunday dinner. Every Friday and Saturday night, however, the scene changed at the cafeteria. These were dance party nights when big dance bands from Houston would come down, and the crowds were loud and boisterous.

The construction workers let their hair down on weekends, and they were joined by a number of lonely soldiers. Policemen were few, and the crowds got pretty tempestuous. Some of the men with a little too much to drink would shoot guns in the air. Fights were frequent on the dance floor and in the street. It was the wild west all over again.

The dances were a big draw for people, even outside of Camp Chemical. Many folks walked to the dance all the way from Velasco, which was then a town of its own. Single girls from Freeport who wanted to join the party would come together as a group, so they could provide protection for each other if necessary.

Jackie Bennett (now Mrs. David Swisher), of Lake Jackson, remembers attending the first grade school at Camp Chemical, located in a converted barracks building. The year was 1942-43. Her teacher was Mrs. Parks. Jackie lived in the Dow Trailer Park, and was bussed with other kids from there to the Camp Chemical School.

Jackie is the daughter of the late J. A. "Shorty" Bennett, who was superintendent of Austin Company's heavy equipment yard and in charge of maintenance and assignment of the heavy equipment. "Shorty" was known to just about everyone who was here at the time, not only through his work for Austin Company, but for his many community activities. He coached young boys to box, and he was also involved in the Miss America preliminary beauty contest. He set up the first local contest under the sponsorship of the Jaycees.

Daughter Jackie remembers her first "temporary" housing in Velasco, which was really just a canvas tent facility. Her memories of Camp Chemical include the huge walkway in front of the general store, which was always busy with hundreds of

CAMP CHEMICAL SCHOOL—This was Mrs. Parks' first grade class at the Camp Chemical School for the 1942-43 term. Can you recognize Jackie Bennett Swisher to whom the photo belongs? She's third from right in back row.

people. She remembers as a child being caught up by the excitement, the energy, and the sense of commitment of everyone connected with the war effort. Everyone knew there was a big job to be done, and she says she always knew things would be better.

When Lake Jackson came along with better housing, the construction force started to decline in numbers, so it was time to close Camp Chemical. In mid-1944, the soldiers left and many unhappy girls remained behind. The cafeteria was closed, and in late 1944, the general store and post office were also closed.

Finally everyone was gone except for a few hard cases who simply refused to move out. It required shutting off the utilities, and even then, a police escort to get the remaining few off the premises. It was constructed strictly as a temporary housing project, and the time had come to say "Adios" to Camp Chemical.

POPULAR PLACE—The Camp Chemical Post Office Lobby was an important place in the early '40s when Dow's first plants were being built. It was not only where one got mail, but also visited with friends and scanned bulletin board notices.

16

Dow Mag Built As Defense Project

LET'S GET back to the construction of Dow Mag, which, by the way, was known as Defense Plant Corporation Project 243.

In the winter of 1941-42, it rained 20 of the 28 days in February. To pour concrete roads, they had to dry the mud with gas burners and then pour the concrete. Finally, it was necessary to move in a pumpcrete machine that mixed concrete in a stationary mixer and pumped the concrete through tubes to the streets. They put the concrete right on top of the mud, and just poured it thicker.

One of the material checkers walked to Hoskins Junction on the railroad to check some material and got lost trying to get back to Dow Mag because of the rain and mud. It was many hours before he was found.

Gazzie McBee, the telephone operator of Plant B, tells of the first temporary telephone shack stuck out in the mud near the Austin Company construction office building. She had to wear rubber boots all the time and walk a boardwalk out to the shack twice a day. A plant security officer was assigned to the telephone shack for protection against intruders.

Many emergency calls had to be put on employees' clock cards

CONSTRUCTION—Dow Chemical Company's Plant B looked like this in the early 1940s.

GAZZIE McBEE— Gazzie McBee was a telephone operator in that period, working in a tiny shack. She now is a Dow mailroom employee.

because there were not enough telephone lines. It was pretty cold in the shack, and Gazzie had only a little electric heater to take away the chill.

There were about 100 truckloads of lumber buried in the mud on Chlorine Road near the Plant B entrance, where there was corduroy road on top of corduroy road.

Mabel Helen Warren, George McGranahan's secretary, went over to Dow Mag even before there were restrooms for women. She had to borrow Ken Rutherford's car to go to Freeport to a restroom. When a ladies' room finally appeared to be ready at the plant, she started to use the room, only to look up and see a workman overhead still working.

*

E. M. Henderson, of the Freeport Sulphur Company, was chairman of the Ration Board. The first month's allocation was only 30 tires for the entire county, and he had 500 applications. The first allocation of gasoline for the county was a trainload! Practically everything was in short supply, even beer. Cigarettes were scarce, and many people who had never smoked before started smoking cigarettes just because they were hard to get.

Meat was also scarce, and had to be rationed. Farmers butchered their own cattle and ate the meat. This gave rise to a number of "Shade Tree Butchers" who probably weren't authentic farmers—but they butchered cattle out under a tree and sold the meat. One well-known "Shade Tree Butcher" operated between Clute and Lake Jackson.

Fresh fruits and vegetables were also scarce. For a while, the Clemens Unit of the Texas Department of Corrections sold some of its produce. It was peddled on the streets of Freeport by enterprising truck owners who brought it to the housewives.

One day a week, the milk truck would pull up to the Freeport Ice House. There would be a line of people two blocks long waiting to buy the milk.

*

Ivan Oden said the Dow Mag Plant, with all its problems, was built by Dow for less than had been estimated—and this was the only DPC plant that operated under the expected cost. All others were over, some of them by enormous amounts.

Oden said that of all the millions of dollars billed to Dow Magnesium Corporation during the construction of Dow Mag, Thiokol, Barge Canal, and Styrene, only one invoice was turned down and not reimbursed to Dow. That was an invoice in the amount of $7.50, for a thermos pitcher to be used for drinking water by McGranahan when he first moved his office to Dow Mag and before there was drinking water available.

At the time Plant B construction was under way, the government plant job at A was finished, and all material and equipment was transferred to Plant B. There were 41 typewritten sheets listing the items at cost. The DPC auditors returned the list to Dow with many dollars of postage on it. They said Dow had failed to add correctly by one cent. Oden rechecked the figures, and found there was no error.

Finding a sufficient work force during the war was a big problem. They needed 10,500 construction workers at Plant B. The government helped. The Army checked all over the country for craftsmen and sent them from Florida, Michigan, and wherever they could find them. Tremendous overtime and good pay helped to keep them here.

During wartime, it was sometimes difficult to keep good communications between the Freeport plants and the home office in Midland, Michigan. One story going the rounds had to do with a report to the home office about putting shell on the canal levee so it could be used for automobile traffic. The message said, "The levee road was shelled today." Back came a quick question—"Did you return fire?"

17

20 and 5 Club
Filled Social Gap

CONTINUING OUR reminiscing about construction of Dow's Plant B, I think we should not forget some of the social activities of the time. First, do you remember the 20 and 5 Club?

The fellows tumbled out of their beds in the Dow barracks early in the morning. It was time to make their own breakfast. They cooked on top of their heater, which was simply an open gas burner boxed in with metal. The top of the box was hot enough to fry eggs and heat water for coffee. To add a bit of local cuisine, they opened a can of beans and heated them to go with the eggs. Bread or packaged sweet rolls completed the breakfast fare which was eaten off of "tin" plates with metal utensils.

This was in the late spring of 1942 when a number of single men were living in the barracks at Plant A. They, along with some other single men working for the Freeport Sulphur Company, found few organized social activities in the Freeport area. So they got together and organized the 20 and 5 Club (so called because there were 25 in the group) and started to make their own entertainment. Some of the original members in the club were: Don Watzke, Bill Weddell, A. C. Burkholder, Maury Havlik and Clyde Boyd of Dow, and Speedy Nelson of the Sulphur Company.

For a time, there was no place to eat except in downtown Freeport and Velasco, so the men made their own breakfast and carried sack lunches that had been prepared at a Freeport cafe the night before. Some nights after work, they drove down to Freeport to play duck pins at an outdoor alley on Broad Street. After a few fast games, it was time to go to the show at the Port Theater. Other nights, they went to the Brown Room on Park Avenue to shoot pool and drink beer.

One or two of the men owned a car. These were the days of gas and tire rationing, and no new cars were being produced, so the men pooled their ration stamps to have enough gas to attend the nighttime affairs.

I asked Don Watzke where the single fellows found the girls for the various parties, dances, etc. He said the girls were daughters of older Dow and Sulphur Company employees, or of businessmen they knew in Freeport and Velasco. Virginia Houston and Mary McLendon (now Graves) were a couple of the girls invited to the social activities of the 20 and 5 Club.

*

It was a big treat to have Sunday dinner on linen tablecloths at the Tarpon Inn in Freeport. The Oaks, located on Highway 36, just east of Jones Creek, hosted many parties. Music for dancing was usually provided by nickelodeons at five cents (yes, five cents) a record, or six plays for a quarter. Since air conditioning was non-existent then, the place was cooled by big exhaust fans.

The top fun spot, though, was the huge Plantation Ballroom in Houston, located where South Main intersects Old Spanish Trail. Big parties featuring name bands were held there on Christmas and New Year's Eve. The ballroom had a porch that extended over the driveway, and you could drive up with your date, get out of the car, and a valet would park your car.

Right next door to the ballroom was a giant amusement park, complete with a roller coaster and many other rides, which gave a carnival atmosphere to the whole location. After a big evening of dancing at the Plantation Ballroom, you could top off the evening with a thrilling ride on the roller coaster.

*

Another big social affair held on New Year's Eve was the Founders Garden Club party at the Freeport Community House. It was THE event of the season and was strictly limited to members, with only a small number of tickets for non-members. All the women wore evening gowns, and usually, out-of-town bands played. I was fortunate to attend one of these glamorous affairs, and it was an unforgettable experience. A description of one of these gala affairs said:

> "One of the most elaborate social events of the Holiday Season was planned at the Freeport Community House. Highlighting a decorative theme that emphasized the colors of blue, white and silver, the mantelpiece held the focal point of interest.
>
> "Its central arrangement of flocked evergreen sprays, silver leaves and berries was flanked with a triad grouping of white tapers in silver candelabras.
>
> "Above the centerpiece was suspended a large cluster of graduated silver and white bells. The bell clusters also were suspended at intervals from the ceiling of the long ballroom.
>
> "Guests were seated at tables upon which large blue foil doilies served to point up elongated arrangements of the flocked evergreens, and silver berries intermingled with bells and white tapers."

Reservations for the Community House could be made not more than one year in advance, and the Garden Club was always quick to get the reservation for the following year. Another group once called in at 8 a.m. on January 2 for a reservation the next New Year's Eve, but the place was already taken!

RECOGNIZE ANYONE?—Above are the officers of the 20 and 5 Club, which was formed back in the early '40s to help fill the recreational gap that existed in Brazosport when people poured into the area to build and operate the Dow plants. Below, club members and their guests go on a picnic.

18

New Product,
New Town Are Born

THE BIGGEST event for Dow Chemical's Texas Division in 1942 was the pouring of the first magnesium from the Plant B facilities in June—less than six months after breaking ground, and several days ahead of an almost impossible schedule. Representatives of the War Department were here, along with top Dow officials, to witness this historic occasion. General Manager A. P. Beutel, was present, of course, and was proud of his crew and all the people who had made this possible. Dr. Willard Dow, president of Dow Chemical, was also on hand, along with representatives of the Office of Production Management and the War Production Board from Washington.

On that eventful day, the first molten magnesium bubbled to the top of the mag pot. Jordie Mariam, production foreman and one of the senior employees at Plant A Magnesium Department, did the honors of dipping the magnesium to make the first ingot in the giant new Plant B magnesium operation. After Mariam poured the magnesium into the molds, the metal hardened and the molds were opened. The first ingots made at the new plant were handed to Beutel and Dow. Thus, another chapter in Dow's astonishing production record was completed.

In 1942, Beutel received a well-earned recognition from his alma mater, The Case Institute of Technology in Cleveland, when the school awarded him an honorary doctorate degree. From then on he was affectionately known as "Dr. Beutel."

By October of 1942, a full-scale Thiokol plant was underway at Plant B to make synthetic rubber. Other plants put into operation by Dow in 1942 were Chlorine 2 and Power 2 at Plant B, and Carbon Tetrachloride and Triethylene Glycol at Plant A.

*

Now I want to tell you a tale about a whole new town to service the employees of the Dow plants. One day soon after Pearl Harbor, Beutel was in his office with Dr. Barstow, Alden Dow and George McGranahan. The discussion turned to talk of a new town to house the thousands of people needed to man the wartime plants. Beutel said, "I know just the place for a new town; come and I'll show you." McGranahan had already scouted the place and had discussed the location with Beutel.

The four headed their car north by northwest. They soon ran out of shell road and picked up a deeply rutted country lane. They bumped along through the swampy, heavily wooded bottomlands along Oyster Creek until Beutel finally came to a point about where the Lone Star Steak House is now located at the corner of Oyster Creek Drive and That Way in Lake Jackson. At that time, however, there was nothing but trees draped with Spanish moss, their shadows hiding rattlesnakes and copperheads. "This is it," Beutel said, and thus the Lake Jackson site was picked and started.

Architect Alden Dow and his family left a comfortable home in Midland, Michigan, and moved down to Freeport so he could take over the design and construction of Lake Jackson. They stayed for three years.

The site was selected for several reasons, including:

> 1. It was far enough inland for protection from Gulf storms, but near enough to the coast to enjoy the beautiful Gulf beaches and deep sea fishing; and,

HISTORIC OCCASION—First magnesium ingots produced at Dow's Texas Division in 1942 are proudly displayed by two government agency representatives from Washington and Dow's A. P. Beutel and Willard Dow, far right.

JORDIE MARIAM—Mariam, left, was production foreman at Plant A Mag cells, but was brought to Plant B to dip the first metal. He is now retired and ranches near West Columbia.

2. The site had an abundance of beautiful
trees, shrubs and other vegetation.

Dow bought 6,500 acres for $400,000. After making
arrangements with the First National Bank in Houston,
McGranahan gave his personal check for $300,000 to the owner,
a Dr. Bertner in Houston, to pay for 5,000 acres of the 6,500-acre
tract.

The project was started in August of 1942. The original plans
called for a town of 3,000 to 4,000 people. The townsite was to
have its own sewer and water systems.

Houses were to be built on lots 60 ft. by 75 ft. wide, and about
140 ft. deep The Federal Public Housing Authority had plans
approved to build 200 houses consisting of one, two, and three
bedroom units, with all utilities. An additional 800 to 1,000 two-
and three-bedroom houses were to be built by private builders.
In order to speed the work, no lots were sold to individuals at
first, as it might have been impossible for them to build under
the wartime regulations.

The townsite had a variety of beautiful trees and shrubs—
sprawling live oaks, huge pecans, colorful yaupons, and holly.
The streets perpetuated their names: Grapevine Turn, Azalea,
Periwinkle Court, Oak Drive, Acacia, Elm, Yaupon, etc.
Winding streets eliminated the monotony of straight rows of
houses. Main avenues had 300-ft. right-of-ways, with 100-ft.
parkways on either side. No buildings faced on these streets.

There were more than 50 different house designs used by the
private builders. Unlike the wartime houses, they had character
and color—all due to Alden Dow.

19

Pride Came
With City's Growth

ORIGINAL PLANS for Lake Jackson included a shopping center adequate to care for the needs of the new town's residents. Alden Dow worked up a layout for these shops that incorporated a protected passage from building to building and provided a generous parking area.

School facilities were carefully considered and a new building was requested for the project. The entire town would provide an ideal location for children, as through traffic would be routed on the main super drives, with residences on quieter, shaded, side avenues. Plans for the project also included many playgrounds and park areas. Adjacent to the lake, there would be up-to-date picnic grounds, which would include a barbeque pit, dance floor and comfort stations. In order to bring the pleasures of Texas close to home for the citizens of the community, there would be public stables and numerous bridle paths opened.

The first sections of the town would be opened at the easterly end of the property, while business areas would be provided near the natural center, along the lines of traffic flow and within walking distance of the homes. Provisions were also made for the establishment of municipal services such as fire and police protection and garbage collection. Early Lake Jackson had its own drug store, grocery store, physician, minister, barber, two home builders, beauty shop, service station, 70-horse riding stable, ice house, sewage and water treatment plants, 100,000-gallon water tower, local stage coach to shuttle people to and from the center of town, telephone exchange, post office, and community center.

The first two- and three-bedroom homes rented for $39.50 and $47.50 per month, respectively. Later these homes would be sold for $4,000 and $5,000.

John Suggs was the very first to move into Lake Jackson on Trumpet Vine in the winter of 1943. He was followed by Grady Dansby, Bob Graves, and Eddie Greenawalt. The weather was cold and rainy. There was no gas connected at first, and the first few days, the occupants were bitterly cold. The streets weren't even finished, but because housing was so badly needed, people came anyway.

There were no clothes dryers in those days, so the clothes had to be hung outside to dry. The mosquitoes were so bad that folks had to hang a few clothes and rush back into the house away from the insects.

Raymond Kelly tells of moving to Lake Jackson in January of 1943. He moved into a three-bedroom duplex that seemed like a palace after the one-bedroom place in Freeport. The new place had a refrigerator, a stove and the works. It was the happiest move he had ever made.

There was no telephone system in Lake Jackson, only rural eight-party lines. Whenever the phone rang, everyone picked it up. Suggs would always say "Hellooo" no matter whose it was.

The first streets were mostly mud, but Oyster Creek Drive was oyster shell. In spite of the rustic appearance, it was obvious that Lake Jackson would be a beautiful site. It would just take a lot of time and effort by the people to make it so. The residents quickly developed a very high civic respect for their new town. Pride actually caused the development of stores and schools. A fire truck was donated to the city by Dow, and was operated by volunteers.

A few of the men got together and visited the Angleton

Jaycees. Shortly thereafter, they had an organization meeting at Suggs' home and formed their own chapter. They elected Suggs to be the first president. Suggs says it was probably because "they were at my home, and I furnished the Cokes."

Meanwhile, things were also happening in Freeport and Velasco. Housing units were being built, including Victory Courts on Ninth and Tenth Streets, the Rainwater houses on Sixth, Seventh, and Eighth Streets, the New River Addition of 209 homes, and the Avalon Construction Company section (180 units in the West Fifth Street area).

In 1943, the Little Theater of Brazosport was organized. Homer and Virginia Beakley, Bob King, Mrs. W. E. Clark, and Elizabeth Oden were some of the organizers. Their first appearance on stage was a one-act comedy, *I'm A Fool*, directed by Elizabeth Oden. This was a part of one of the community choral programs.

Next about a dozen people pooled $10 each to make and

THREE R's —First building constructed for a school in Lake Jackson was on what is now the Elisabeth Ney campus. Here it is obviously recess time for the new city's students.

produce a show. They had no building, so they used Mrs. Clark's back yard and vacant garage. Young bachelors living at Mrs. Clark's boarding house made and painted the sets. She furnished the workers coffee and fresh homemade donuts. In 1943, at the Freeport High School, they put on a three-act play, *Ice Bound*, again directed by Elizabeth Oden.

In 1944 a constitution and state charter were drawn up. After many years of successful plays, in 1952 an old house on Front Street in Velasco was purchased and the theater had a home.

EARLY ORIGINS—A new town is born and the workers leaving the construction shack are making it possible. Those same trees may now be shading some Lake Jackson home. John Suggs was one of the earliest residents to move into the young town. Now retired, Suggs lives outside the city on the lake shore at Lake Jackson Farms.

20

1943 Brought 'E' Award, Tornado

IN THE spring of 1943, within only three weeks of opening, the Dow Chemical Texas Division Thiokol Plant was ordered to shut down construction. By this time, a newer and better synthetic rubber was becoming available.

The Thiokol or Polysulphide rubber became brittle in cold weather. This was one of the reasons the Germans were defeated in Russia. The Germans' tires would burst in the cold and bog down their mobile equipment.

A new Dow product to go on stream in 1943 at Plant A was chloroform.

*

In May of 1943, two big celebrations were held at the Dow plants. The prestigious Army-Navy "E" (for excellence) Award was given to Dow Texas Division. On the same day, the Dow Magnesium Corporation at Plant B also received an Army-Navy "E" Award.

The Plant B presentation was in the morning, with C. M Shigley, assistant general manager of DMC, acting as master of ceremonies. Dr. E. W. Bennett, president of Dow Magnesium Corporation, was there to accept the award for Dow. Rear

Admiral P. W. Foote, U. S. Navy, presented the company award. Colonel Royden Williamson, U. S. Army, presented pins to the following employee representatives: John Hrncir, Magnesium Chloride Department; L. B. McGaughey, Magnesium Cells; J. L. Kight, Service Department; and, Kingdon Browning, Boiler Shop. Colonel Williamson said, "The 'E' pins and award stand not only for excellence, but also for the energy you have expended in establishing the records which have earned them."

The program included music by the Dow Band under the direction of Jerry Bryan, posting of the colors by the Military Police detachment in Freeport, raising the award flag, and an acceptance speech by Dr. Bennett. In his address, Dr. Bennett said, "This is more than a war plant. In the peace to come, it will contribute enormously to the nation's prosperity and comfort."

In the afternoon, the big celebration moved to Plant A for the "E" Award presentation to the Texas Division of Dow. G. M. McGranahan, assistant general manager, was master of ceremonies. A. P. Beutel, general manager of the Texas Division, accepted the company award. Pins for the Texas Division employees were accepted by V. L. Loughry, Ethylene; O. C. Dunaway, Magnesium Chloride; L. O. Newborn, Service; J. C. Biggs, Magnesium Cells, and Joe Malone, Boiler Shop.

Rear Admiral P. W. Foote said, "These two Texas Dow plants have not only maintained full production, but have doubled the production for which they were originally designed. This latter was the deciding factor in making the awards."

A. P. Beutel said, "We have one outstanding advantage, and this is, conversion from war efforts to peacetime pursuits should take place without interruption."

*

In September, the first issue of the DOW TEXAN was published, with Ednale Martin co-editor.

The Dow cafeterias started sending lunch wagons into the plants dispensing hot lunches with sandwiches, soup, chili, stew, baked beans, pie, candies, and hot coffee. These were welcomed by the workers who were too far from the cafeterias to get a hot meal at noon.

*

The Division was shut down for a hurricane from October 16-19, 1943. Eighteen special busses were run to Houston by Missouri Pacific Lines to carry people to safety. Some 2,000 Dow people spent three days in the Houston Coliseum during the hurricane. Dow's Jim Hiner was the shelter manager at the Coliseum.

In November 1943, the first tornado that anyone could remember hit Freeport. Edith Tobey (now Davenport) tells that it became pitch dark at 3 p.m. Then the tornado came in just before dusk, moving in from the open Gulf, following an irregular path and more or less parallel to the Missouri Pacific tracks. It jumped the Brazos River near the railroad bridge and dissipated into the prairie a few miles north of the city after severing all telephone and power lines serving Freeport and Velasco.

Freeport was isolated for a short time with all lines of communication down and a static field of such intensity that prevented any radio reception. The disaster had occurred in a matter of seconds, killing two people and injuring scores of others. Property damage was $400,000.

The tornado ripped several houses from their foundations in Victory Courts addition, then struck an elementary school two blocks away. Next it came to the residential section leveling many buildings and sweeping others from their foundations. The storm passed the Catholic and Presbyterian Churches, but flattened the social hall of the Catholic Church. One house was lifted from its foundation and smashed onto the home of a neighbor across the street.

George T. Wommack, Sr., a Freeport resident at the time, describes one of the strange effects of the tornado. A small grocery store on Second Street was in the path, and all four walls were opened up and laid back on the ground, leaving the groceries intact on the shelves. One thing was hard to understand, however. All the stuffed olives in glass bottles had the pimento stuffing sucked out of the olives and pulled to the top of the bottles without the caps being removed.

EXCELLENCE—Joe Biggs gets award pin from Col. Williamson for Dow Plant A Mag employees for wartime effort. Biggs, now retired, still lives in Lake Jackson. Above, the Army-Navy 'E' flag flew over plants in '43.

TRAGEDY—Two people died in the tornado that left this kind of damage in the city of Freeport in November, 1943, as the town was full of people concerned with getting the new Dow facilities into production.

21

Horseback Riding Was Popular Lake Jackson Sport

IN OCTOBER of 1943, Lake Jackson had its first big celebration with a street dance sponsored by the Jaycees. Alden Dow, who had drawn the plans for the city, was interested and paid for a big band which played for the street dance. Logs were burning in the background from the clearing operations, and it was a beautiful scene. John Suggs, president of the Jaycees, gave a speech which described Lake Jackson, for the first time, as the "City of Enchantment." The speech had been written by Art Webb, owner of the Lake Drug Store, who was later called "Mr. Lake Jackson."

Also in October, the Lake Jackson Riding Club took its first ride of the season from the corral at Lake Jackson to Flag Lake and back. Riders in the group included the Warsings, the Colegroves, the Odens, and the Suggses. The Riding Club had actually been organized the preceding November, after Dow started clearing the land for the city of Lake Jackson. Gas and tire rationing had made it necessary that people find entertainment nearby so they wouldn't need to use their automobiles. Also, a lot of us were just drug store cowboys who came to the Southwest from Michigan and jumped at the chance to put on some cowboy boots and a hat, and climb on a cayuse for a ride.

Other early members in the Club included the Ernie Holdens, the Earl Collinses, the Truman Devores, the Pete Gurklises, the George Greenes, the Oliver Beutels, the J. P. Warrens, and the Roy Barringers.

Dow had been using horses in the Plant B Security Patrol. As this Patrol closed down, some of the horses were put out at the Lake Jackson corral where the Dow Pavilion is now located. George Edwards, who was later security officer for the city of Lake Jackson under "Cap" Brown, looked after the horses and ran the Club for a time. Later, Dempsey Montgomery and his wife, Helen, ran the Club and the stables.

Several people bought their own horses and left them at the Club. Dr. A. P. Beutel owned a beautiful quarter horse named Lucille. Lewis Warsing's horse was Rex, and Judy Warsing's was Queen. Some of the rent horses' names were Shorty Closs, Turkey, Charley, and Ginger. Turkey was the one to use when just learning to ride. However, if you wanted some spirit and felt adventurous, you could try a ride on Ginger.

Harland Sherbrook and Lewis Warsing used to ride their horses on a complete tour of the Lake Jackson housing construction job every Sunday. Sometimes the women would go out in the middle of the week and take their lunch. Often they would go on a five-mile trip around the lake, which was a very pretty ride. The Warsings and the Holdens rode nearly every weekend to Brazoria and to Angleton.

One ride that was popular was out along the levee and then down from the levee through the woods to Flag Lake, where the riders often had a picnic. It was quite a long ride for greenhorns, however, and many rode horses out and came back in a pickup. The hardier souls led the riderless horses, sometimes as many as seven or eight, back to the Club.

Another popular ride was to the old syrup mill. It was out in the pasture towards Brazoria near McFadden's Slough, north of what is now Highway 332. There was a lot of brickwork still left from when the syrup mill was used as part of the old Lake Jackson Plantation.

I think my fondest memories of this Riding Club, however,

were the Sunday morning breakfasts on the trail. Earl Collins was entertainment chairman, and he arranged several of these outings. We would start out on horseback about 7 a.m. Earl would go on ahead and get the fire started. By the time we arrived at the breakfast site, Earl had coffee ready in the 15-gallon aluminum kettle, and was frying up bacon and eggs for the hungry riders. After a delicious breakfast in the open air, we would mount up and continue our ride through the forest, getting back to the corral a little before noon.

In 1944, there were 368 adult members in the Riding Club. There were 21 horses for rent, and 47 privately owned horses. The Sherbrooks owned four horses, one for each member of the family. A single membership cost $2.50 a year, and a family membership was $5. Horses rented for 50¢ the first hour, and 35¢ for each additional hour.

The toughest activity I remember about the Club was building the corral, which the members worked on during weekends. We used live oak timbers for the corral fence, and the wood was so hard we had to drill holes first before we could drive nails. The wives were on hand to provide coffee and lunches for the workers.

When World War II ended, and as gasoline and tires became more available, the Riding Club started to decline. A symbol of the Old West quietly faded from the scene.

LAKE JACKSON RIDING CLUB—This corral was built by its members—near the lake, close to where the Dow Pavilion and barbecue pits are now located.

CLUB BOSS—George Edwards, an authentic western cowboy, ran the Lake Jackson Riding Club which flourished in the early '40s as Dow's first plants went on stream.

22

Jaycees Formed In 1943

THE COMMUNITY of Lake Jackson began to be noticed in 1943. In March, the first grocery store, a Piggly Wiggly store, opened. Jimmie Carroll and L. C. Morrison took over ownership soon after. A Humble service station was opened at the corner of Center Way and South Parking Place. It was not long before Burley Schmidt took over the service station, where he and his family took good care of our automobiles for a long time.

The first telephone switchboard opened in April. Dorothy Kelly (Mrs. Raymond) was the operator for a time. In June, the Proctor Walgreen Drug Store (later to be the Lake Drug Store) opened under the ownership of Art Webb.

Annette Greer was the first postmistress in Lake Jackson when that service opened in November. Before that, volunteer workers, including the Jaycees, would go to the Dow Trailer Park Post Office to pick up the mail. Then it would be distributed at an office on South Parking Place to residents who would come there every afternoon.

The Jaycees were the first men's civic group organized in Lake Jackson. They received their charter on October 22, 1943. John Suggs was the first president. Other members were   L. F.

Grafius, T. J. Dunbar, Jr., Wallace Corbin, G. D. Burns, Dr. R. C. Miller, J. F. Unerfusser, W. L. May, L. H. Bowers, Glenn Harris, H. T. Youens, G. M. Lindveit, A. C. Ray, Lee Norris, Jr., C. R. Green, W. B. Gibson, and F. G. Akers.

The Federal Public Housing Administration built 200 duplex units in Lake Jackson, as well as a community house located between Winding Way and Center Way. This was the only place we had for meetings, and various groups met there. Most Protestant faiths met together for church and Sunday school in the Community House. Also, just about every Saturday night the building was used for a big party. When Sunday morning came, some of the ushers would come early to pick up the beer bottles and get the place ready for church.

This was the time of the Victory Gardens in both Freeport and Lake Jackson. To help boost the food supply, the Freeport Sulphur Company and Dow made some land available in Freeport and Lake Jackson, respectively, for growing vegetables. Many people also had Victory Gardens in their own backyards. Pete Gurklis took first place in a Victory Garden contest that year.

In the early '40s, there was a landmark in Velasco that most everyone who was here at the time will remember. It was Martin's Grocery & Market, located on the spot where the Texaco station now stands near the intersection of Brazosport and Gulf Boulevards. There was no Highway 288 there at the time. When you came across the levee road at the end of the harbor, you would run right into Martin's before turning east on Gulf Boulevard.

Zella Martin tells of how the store came to be built. Robert Martin, a brother of Zella's husband, Bill, bought the land in 1941. He figured there would be development to the west and it would be a good investment for a general store. Robert and his mother, Winifred Martin, built Martin's Grocery & Market and moved their stock from a store in Sandy Point to Velasco, opening the store in January of 1942. Meanwhile, Robert joined the Air Force soon after Pearl Harbor, and was reported shot down over Germany in 1943, and missing in action.

Zella and Winifred Martin ran the store for several years. They stocked clothes of all kinds for men and women, including

JAYCEES AT WORK

JAYCEES—The club formed in 1943 in Lake Jackson and it is still in operation. Pictured are some of the early members.

GARDEN PROJECT—Victory gardens were being encouraged by the federal government throughout the land. In Lake Jackson, residents of the town struggled with the gumbo to do their wartime duty as seen above.

gloves, caps, pants, and shirts. They also carried hardware and a full line of groceries and fresh meats. The store was open from 7 a.m. until 7 p.m. six days a week, and closed on Sunday. In the late '50s, the store was closed down, but not until it had been a landmark for a long time during the war years.

Another place I remember during the '40s was the Baytex Hotel dining room in Bay City. We went there for the first time for Sunday dinner after church with the Ivan Odens. At that time, their dining room was one of the newest and best eating places around, even matching the better spots in Houston. It was a real pleasure to sit down to an old fashioned Sunday dinner of fried chicken, mashed potatoes, caramel rolls and dessert, all homemade, and elegantly served in a beautiful setting.

A FAMILIAR LANDMARK—Remembered by many who were here in Dow's early days was Martin's store in Velasco, which was then a city of its own. (It later became the portion of Freeport north of the river.)

23

Couples Club
Keeps On Dancing

DAMON RUNYON tells of the oldest continuous permanent floating crap game in New York. Let me tell you of the oldest continuous permanent dance club in Brazosport, and probably in the country.

In the early '40s, a number of couples who had been sent down from Michigan by Dow, started the Couples Dance Club. These included the Harland Sherbrooks, the Oliver Beutels, the Herman Schmidts, the Colegroves, and the Reichenbachs. They were joined by the Si DeZavalas, the Red Dodsons, the Joe Powells, and the Stan Rushs. Later, the Ken Rutherfords, the John Suggses and others also joined the Club. There wasn't much entertainment in Freeport, so this served as a social affair to get together with friends from the North, as well as new local friends.

The Club met once a month, the year round, at the Freeport Community House. In the early days, liquor was not allowed in the Community House, so those who wanted to drink would go out to their cars. John Suggs remembers that several were chastised for going to the car too often.

Live bands were used most of the time, except when the

treasury got low, and then there would be dancing to a nickelodeon. In the middle '40s, we used Phil DiGuardi's band a lot. His first group included Phil on sax and clarinet, Stan Smock on trumpet, Howard Dilts on piano, and Johnny Robbins on string bass.

Phil soon added a cute French singer, then recently from Paris, Mickie Fuller. She was married to Jack Fuller, Dr. A. P. Beutel's secretary. At that time, the band all wore French tams and were called Four Notes and a Song. Still later, Phil's band included Gene Markley, Grant Scoggins, Stan Gamble, Andy Anderson, and a few others who sat in from time to time.

The jitterbug style of dance was popular in the '40s and early '50s. *Sioux City Sue* was a great number to jitterbug to.

As time passed in the '40s, Gus and Frances Lindveit, Joe and Lenora Mitchell, and E. A. and Arlene Penney showed up at the dances. In 1946, Emil and Augusta Richter joined. They came from Garwood near El Campo. They said the Club reminded them of the old community dance halls back home. The Richters are still members of the Dance Club which ties together a span from the '40s to the '80s, or over 40 years of continuous Dance Club existence.

Some of the stylish lady dancers who will be remembered are Augusta Richter, Mollie Luckenbach, Arlene Penney and Lenora Mitchell. The late E. A. Penney may be best remembered of the men dancers. He always ended with a beautiful flourish and a lay back of the lady almost to the floor, as he swept one hand in a wide arc as a salute to the audience. Penney was without a doubt a dance king, and all the ladies liked to be picked by him for a dance. Phil Di Guardi says Penney's fashionable dance was a trademark of the '40s and '50s, and a famous ballroom style.

One year when Ernie Rea was president of the Club, he and I used to provide a special little game or skit at each dance. We'd pull this off at the second intermission when everyone was fairly mellow and almost anything would be received with great applause. One of our productions, *Dirty Work at the Crossroads*, featured Ernie as the villain, and Opal Walker as the beautiful damsel. I was the sheriff. There hadn't been time to practice, so we used big cue cards.

One of our dances featured a Sadie Hawkins Day theme, and everyone came appropriately dressed. Prizes were given for the best costumes. Opal Walker won as Daisy Mae, Jerrie Goebel as Mammy Yokum, Dr. Jack Taylor as Pappy Yokum, and Sena Colegrove as Moonbeam McSwine.

Many exciting events occurred at the dances over the years. One night a lady slipped and fell on her face on the well-waxed floor. Her two front teeth were each bent back out of alignment. Dentist Jack Taylor, who was one of the guests, immediately came forward and had the patient removed to the kitchen. There he proceeded to bring both teeth back into alignment by the use of his thumb. Ernie Rea said this was Dr. Taylor's finest hour, and that this was the only time whiskey was used both as an anesthetic and an antiseptic. The lady reported later that

POPULAR MUSICMAKER—New Orleans was where Phil DiGuardi honed his musical talents but Brazosport has been where he has done most of his entertaining. The affable DiGuardi's bands played for many social events in the early Dow days. Retired now from Dow, DiGuardi still lives in Lake Jackson and in recent years has played with Brazosport College musical groups.

evening that   her teeth were back to normal in every respect.

In the early days, we went to the Freeport Grill about 1:30 a.m. for breakfast after the dances. In the later years, we went to Bennett's, an all-night restaurant on Highway 288 in Clute. A few times, breakfast was served at the Community House after the dance.

The Dance Club was very popular, and there was usually a waiting list to get in. Sometimes it took as long as three or four months to get in. The members couldn't even bring guests most of the time because the dance would be too crowded.

After 40 years, the Dance Club still meets—the oldest continuous dance club still goes on.

24

Drug Store Was
Town Social Center

THE SIGN in the window read: "Open from 8 a.m. till 10 p.m. seven days a week. Closed Christmas Day." This was the old Lake Drug Store in downtown Lake Jackson when it was owned and managed by Art Webb.

The store was opened in 1943 as Proctor Walgreen Drug by Art Webb and D'Orville Evans. Webb and Evans also owned Walgreen Drug Store in Freeport. When the partnership later split, and each took one of the stores, Webb kept the Lake Jackson store.

The late Harold Monical told about the drug store in 1945, after he'd returned from the armed services. It was the hub of the community, and thus a meeting place for most of the Lake Jackson residents. One would get all the local news by visiting the drug store. Many business transactions also took place there over coffee. Monical and J. C. Powell were in business together repairing houses, and since they didn't have an office, they met with their clients at the Lake Drug and carried on business.

Webb had a tremendous sense of humor and was always smiling. He tried to have something on all who came in the store so he could play jokes on them. He was an inveterate cigarette

LAKE DRUG—The fountain area was the social center for Lake Jackson, giving residents of the small town a pleasant place to refresh themselves and visit with friends.

smoker (of Piedmont cigarettes), and he often sat on the corner stool of the drug store fountain with a cup of coffee in one hand and a cigarette in the other. From his "throne" he could see everyone who came in, and he always had a quick greeting for each customer.

Evening habitues of the Lake Drug included Red Leinen, Grady Dansby, Harlow Bellinger, Fred Latham, George Driskill, and Harold Monical. Eventually the group gathered there most every Saturday at 9 a.m. Webb used to accuse some of his regulars of flipping their coffee charge tickets in back of the register so they wouldn't have to pay (coffee was five cents a cup, with free refills).

One day a scroungy, mangy dog appeared on the street outside of the drug store with a big sign which read, "I'm Art Webb's dog, he won't feed me." This was a little retaliation against Webb by his pharmacist because of the unmerciful kidding he had been receiving from Webb.

One of the first to have a television set in Lake Jackson was Art

Webb. He bought it from Foley's in Houston. When it was unpacked at his home one afternoon, Webb invited a number of guests to watch television that night. He hadn't had a chance to check out the set, and that evening after all the guests had arrived, he discovered the TV set didn't have any works—it was an empty wooden cabinet. First thing the next morning, the telephone lines were burning to Foley's in Houston.

Webb never had dinner at night until after the store closed at 10 p.m. He would go home and his wife, Elizabeth, would then cook and serve dinner. However, some nights he and Harlow Bellinger, with whom Webb was constantly playing chess, would be in the middle of a game when it was time to close the store. They finished many a game in the back room after closing.

Art Webb was very community minded, having been the first president of The Lake Jackson Bank, president of the Lake Jackson Businessmen's Association and the Brazosport Chamber of Commerce, vice president of the Texas State Softball Association, president of the elite President's Club, as well as many other offices of leadership. He was a religious person—a Catholic. Unknown, to but a few, he gave lots of medicine to people who couldn't afford to buy it.

ART WEBB—Webb, left, peeks over packages at his Lake Drug with wife Elizabeth by him and pharmacist Hartman and his wife at right.

Art Webb died in 1953. He was in Lake Jackson only about 10 years, but he had an enormous affect on the business and recreational life of the little city of Lake Jackson. His friends are legion, and he will long be remembered as "Mr. Lake Jackson."

*

Soon after moving into Lake Jackson in early 1943, the first bridge club was formed by the early residents on Trumpet Vine. Dorothy Kelly and Hazel Gill helped start the club.

A Women's Club was formed in Lake Jackson in late 1943, sparked by Cornelia Lee, the activities director of the Federal Public Housing Authority's 200 duplex units. Some of the early members were Dorothy Kelly, Carol Ray, Hazel Gill, Ruby Youens, Sena Colegrove, Sue Greer, and Vera Dunbar. The ladies would bring a pot luck lunch and meet all day at the Community House in the duplex area. Many also brought their children along. They worked on various activities and programs for the community.

I remember at one of the Women's Club parties they had a men's beauty contest to pick the man with the most beautiful legs—Miss "Legs" Jackson. Homebuilder A. C. Ray won the contest hands down with his shapely, but oh so hairy legs.

In 1946, the Women's Club distributed its first cookbook. It is still considered a source of the best recipes by some Lake Jackson residents. Sena Colegrove says she uses Mrs. J. S. "Cap" Brown's recipe for pecan pie, and has yet to find another recipe as good.

The Women's Club was the springboard for the Lake Jackson Garden Club, which has had a resplendent history, and is still active today. Their first flower show, held in the Community House of the duplex area, was a success, due in no small part to Dow's donation of several hundred dollars' worth of shrubs that were used as prizes.

HELEN THOMPSON—Hostess for an early Lake Jackson Garden Club show was Helen Thompson, right, who poses with Dorothy Kelly, left, and Jack Wilson.

25

Dow Hospital
Opened With 42 Beds

IN THE year 1942, with the big push on to build the Dow Mag plant, the hospital situation became acute. The Freeport Clinic and Hospital simply was not large enough to take care of the need for hospital services. So the 42-bed Dow Magnesium Hospital was constructed and opened in August of 1942.

By September, the early staff consisted of a Dr. Cecil, Dr. Bob Miller, Dr. S. B. Slaughter, and Pauline Beauchamp as director of nurses. Frank Smith was business manager, and Ralph Riggan was maintenance superintendent.

Ilene Scott (now Mrs. Floyd Sharp) tells of the early days of the hospital. She joined the nursing staff in October of 1942 as a staff nurse. She was later promoted to supervisor of the emergency and operating rooms. In 1951, she was made director of nursing services where she served until her retirement in 1964.

The spanking new hospital, with a capacity of 42 beds, was something to be proud of. It had a modern, well-equipped operating room and emergency room, a complete kitchen and dining room for the medical staff of doctors and nurses, and its own laundry. Soon after opening, Dow installed a complete dentistry office and equipped it. Dr.Swanson, a dentist, was engaged to look after the dental care of the employees.

Dr. Cecil left after a short time. Drs. Miller and Slaughter treated the industrial cases in the beginning, later adding a private caseload. Drs. Rayan and Skarke from Freeport were also early doctors helping with industrial cases.

Since housing was so bad, 13 federal government trailers were brought over to the hospital area for housing of nurses. Ilene Scott Sharp remembers several unmarried single nurses who were living in the trailers, including Irene Malchor (now Mrs. Bob Munzy), Essie Mae Wiley (now Mrs. Chives Evans), Frances Mead (now Mrs. Dave Landsborough), Dorothy Wooley (now Mrs. George Caldwell), Pawnee Cox (now Mrs. Gene Holbert), Esther Dascher (now Mrs. T. J. Walker), and a married nurse, Betty Holt.

While living in the trailers was certainly better than most other options, there were still some troublesome features. Two women were assigned to each trailer. They had electricity and heat, but had to walk over to the hospital for showers and to eat their meals. The nurses lived in the trailers from October of 1942 until March of 1944, when a new nurses' home was built for them.

The new home had 12 semi-private rooms, with two women to a room, a community bath with showers, a little kitchenette, a laundry room, and a large living room. Maid service was also provided. Each night the maid would bring food and supplies from the hospital to stock the kitchenette and laundry. While it was convenient for the nurses on the night shift to make snacks in the kitchenette, most meals were still eaten at the hospital.

The single nurses met their dates in the living room before going out on the town. Because of the wartime restrictions, the girls had a midnight curfew. Dow's Plant Protection had a horse patrol that kept a close watch on the nurses' home. If they saw lights on past midnight, the patrol would call "lights out!"

Almost no cars were available, so nurses who were off duty would hitch-hike to Freeport and meet at Brockenbrough's Drug Store on the corner of Broad and Park Avenue. Sometimes they shopped in Freeport, and other times, they'd catch a bus to Houston for a day of shopping. Occasionally, the nurses would use a taxi, riding six at a time.

Ilene Sharp recalls that the paychecks came from the U. S. Government. The hospital was part of Defense Plant Corporation Project No. 243, which was owned by the government, but operated by Dow.

After the 1943 tornado that went through Freeport, the doctors and nurses from the Dow Mag Hospital went to the Freeport Hospital to render first aid and help evacuate the patients to the Dow Mag Hospital. The staff worked continuously around the clock until all the patients were taken care of.

During a hurricane in the late '40s, all the cooks, maids, aides, and some of the nurses left the hospital. The remaining nurses had to perform patient care, janitorial work, cooking and serving of meals, and washing dishes.

The Dow Mag Hospital had a fine record of service. Dr. Mark Thompson became hospital administrator in 1943, and Dr. Bob Miller was chief of staff from 1943 until 1955. In 1944, the hospital was appointed as a depot for the new wonder drug, penicillin, because of the war production here. Only a very few depots were set up because of the scarcity of penicillin at the time.

Dow bought the hospital from the government when Plant B was purchased. The hospital was later given to the community to be administered by a local non-profit hospital association.

DOW MAG HOSPITAL—The new hospital looked like this back in the early '40s .

HOSPITAL STAFF—Early Dow Mag Hospital staff members assembled in front of the building for a photo with Drs. Cecil, Slaughter, and Miller in the front row, with Business Manager Frank Smith at right.

26

Lake Jackson Stagecoach Was Fun and Practical

ONE PHASE of the terrible housing problem that the building of the Dow plants had brought to Brazosport was solved in March of 1944, when the Federal Public Housing Authority opened a new dormitory for women. It was conveniently located in downtown Freeport with facilities for 36 residents. The dormitory offered a nice new and comfortable home, at a reasonable rent, to women working at the Dow plants.

*

Meanwhile in 1944, some innovative Lake Jackson businessmen conceived the idea of a horse-drawn stagecoach to carry people from their homes to and from the downtown business area, and to carry children to the day school at the Community Center. A. C. Ray, one of those businessmen, tells how it began:

> "We were in the middle of gas rationing and food rationing; also we were building a new town and needed to interest people to live in Lake Jackson. Then, it took just about every gas stamp to drive back and forth to work at the Dow Plant. We needed a new idea to sell Lake Jackson, and also to be useful to the residents there."

117

Ray said the idea of using horses came to them after seeing horses pulling the equipment to clear the streets to allow construction of the new homes. The men decided to build a stagecoach to transport people back and forth to the shopping area.

First, they found a lumber dolly and remodeled it by fitting it with axles and car wheels with rubber balloon tires. They had to go to the Ration Board in Angleton to get permission to buy the tires. Then a tongue was put on the front of the dolly in order to hitch up a team of horses. A platform was built on the dolly, and rows of seats were put on both sides, with an aisle in the center. A platform step was built on the back for ease of mounting to the seat platform.

As the hot summer was just beginning, a colorful striped canvas top was mounted on the coach to keep off the direct rays of the sun. Then a pair of black draft horses was found to draw the coach, and Pop Crumrine was hired to be the driver. Pop had driven horses on a farm, and he turned out to be a friendly, careful driver, beloved by all the kids, as well as the adults.

The next thing was to set up a route for the stagecoach. Two routes were planned, leaving the shopping center every 45 minutes from 8:30 a.m. until 4:15 p.m., going alternately by the "northern route" and the "southern route."

The northern route left the drug store, traveling via North Parking Place, Winding Way, Camellia, and again to Winding Way back to the theater, and on to the drug store. The southern route left the drug store and went via Center Way, Oak Drive, Circle Way, Azalea, Magnolia, and again to Center Way back to the drug store. The charge was five cents for kids and 10 cents for adults each way.

Mrs. J. S. "Cap" Brown remembers riding the coach with her neighbor, Mrs. Hugh Metz. It was a pleasant trip to town and back again with everyone laughing and talking.

Folks would get off at the Lake Drug Store and have coffee while visiting with their friends. The Piggly Wiggly Grocery Store was right next door, and many women waited until the grocery supply trucks came in so they could get in line to get rationed foods.

Marilyn Manning (formerly Colegrove) tells of riding on the

stagecoach. The kids didn't want to get on the coach while it was stopped. It was a big thrill for them to wait until it was in motion and then run and jump on the back step. Then they would ride downtown to wait at the Piggly Wiggly Store for the candy truck to come for its delivery of the scarce Butterfingers, Hershey Bars, etc. They knew what day the truck was due, and they were always on hand to get the candy.

Some of the boys and girls who rode the southern route were Susan Shelley, Emily Davidson, and Judy and Jimmy Myers, whose father was in the service in Hawaii.

Ray said the stagecoach idea worked for a number of months, but they finally had to give it up. The metal horseshoes would wear out fast on the concrete pavement, and rubber horseshoes were not available since rubber went for the war effort. Also, since there were simply no blacksmiths to be found, Ray and T. J. Dunbar had to shoe the horses every Sunday. They finally got tired of it, and thus, a great idea finally folded.

THE LAKE JACKSON STAGECOACH

DORMITORY LIFE—Residents of a women's dormitory built in Freeport pursue some leisure interests of reading and visiting.

27

*Lake Jackson
Became City In 1944*

THE YEAR 1944 rolled around. The city of Lake Jackson was incorporated in April, with C. H. Leak as the first mayor. The streets, parks, water and sewer systems, as well as the fire equipment, were given to the city by the Dow Chemical Co.

The first chief of police was Captain J. S. "Cap" Brown, who had served during construction of the city as a deputy for Alden B. Dow, Inc. Brown served the city with distinction, first as city marshall, and later as chief of police for 18 years. He died while still in office.

June 6, 1944, World War II's D-Day in Europe, marked the first edition of the *Lake Jackson News*. Mr. and Mrs. G. M. Lindveit were the owners and publishers. The first issue carried a "Ration Reminder" which stated:

> —Gasoline coupon A-11 was good for three gallons of gas and would expire June 21.
> —Airplane stamp No. 182 was good for one pair of shoes.
> —Sugar stamps No. 30 and 31 were good indefinitely.

> —Certificates were necessary for automobiles, stoves, bicycles, rubber footwear, etc.

A short time after the *Lake Jackson News* began publishing, the publishers of the old *Velasco World* began another newspaper for Lake Jackson known as the *Lake Jackson Roundup*. The masthead featured a cowboy on a galloping horse with a lariat in "full bloom" ready for the lasso. The *Roundup* was fairly short-lived, however. The publishers never took out a mailing permit and it was thrown free to the residents until it went out of business.

Here I would like to make mention of some of the early business and professional residents of Lake Jackson: Dr. R. C. Miller; drug store owner, Art D. Webb; barber, Tom Vaughan; grocer, J. E. Carroll; and, gas station operator, Burley Schmidt. Others included Claire Smith, owner of the Smart Shop (started in her home on Trumpet Vine), which later became Lateer's Dress Shop and in 1945, became LaVelle Shop; T. J. Dunbar, manager of the Lake Jackson Company department of Dow; S. T. McKnight of McKnight Cleaners; A. C. Ray of Plantation Development Co.; Ivan Greer of Brazoria Investment Co.; Howard Bowen and Charley Ohlrogge of Bowen-Ohlrogge Hardware; John Hoopes of Lariat Book Store; and Gayle Douglas of Gayle's Beauty Shop.

Now let's take a brief look at a few of the other things that were happening in the Lake Jackson area in the year of 1944:

In the summer, there was a shortage of refrigeration, so Art Webb installed a big ice house at the corner of This Way and That Way, near his Lake Drug Store.

In July, the Lake Jackson Municipal Airport was certified by the CAA. Runways were mowed to a length of 2,500 feet. Twenty-two cross-country flights were recorded the first weekend. William A. King was the first airport manager.

Three hundred Dow employees were listed in military service for their country. Nine had given their lives.

In August, an election was called for the consolidation of the Freeport, Velasco, and Clute School Districts. The election was held on August 26, and the consolidation passed.

J. S. "CAP" BROWN—"Cap" Brown served as Lake Jackson's first peace officer, as marshal in the early days and later as the chief of police until his death.

THE FIRST—Burley Schmidt operated Lake Jackson's first service station. Around the corner to the right was Lake Drug, which later encompassed the gas station site.

ALDEN B. DOW AND VISITORS—Frank Steves, engineer T. J. Dunbar Jr., architect Alden Dow, in the early days in Lake Jackson.

The Brazosport Chamber of Commerce was organized in October of 1944. The first president was Dr. R. G. Carlton. This took the place of the old Freeport-Velasco Chamber of Commerce which was dissolved the following year.

The Dow Hotel also added an attractive dining room soon after the hotel was built. Virginia Robbins and her harp were featured in the hotel dining room.

In February of 1945, Dow requested the Missouri Pacific to provide bus service from West Columbia, Angleton, Lake Jackson, Freeport and Velasco for Dow employees on all three shifts. Even with the bus service, there was the problem of long travel time. Mildred Schaer remembers riding a bus from West Columbia to work at Plant A. She left West Columbia at 5 a.m. and arrived at Dow about 7 a.m.

The previous September had seen a decrease in magnesium production at Dow Mag. But by the summer of 1945, the plant was requested by the War Department to increase the magnesium production again, so a great number of employees were rehired. Fifty house trailers arrived at the Dow Trailer Park, with additional trailers expected. Because of the Dow Mag start up and new employees being hired, more housing was needed.

A number of women were also hired to work in the plants. Some of them in the Chlorine Maintenance Department included Mary O'Berry, mother of three; Jean Wilson, mother of two; Raye Baker, grandmother; Ollie Marshall, mother of three; and Thelma Leggett, who looked after a cow and chickens on her "farm" after work. Other women worked as plasterers in Mag Cells, and as painters.

That summer the canning kitchen in Freeport was going full blast in the IOOF Lodge Hall under the direction of Mrs. D. V. Collins. Here the fruits of the Victory Garden were being canned.

28

Styrene Dances
Topped Social Year

IN 1945, an interesting group was organized by the name of "Styrene Technical Foreman's Social and Athletic Association"—STFSAA for short. It all started when the Zzlych (yes, Zzlych) boys gave a beach party. These young men were all single, and when they gave their telephone number, they said it was the last name in the book.

The Zzlych boys were better known as Ted Walker, John Keselik, John Ennis, and Bill Newcomb. Walker promoted a beach party for Styrene people featuring roast pig. About 25 people attended, and the party went over so well, the participants decided to have an all-Styrene Department organization. Several of the group were athletically inclined and thought they should include athletic events along with the social events. The organization was to include all salaried employees of the Styrene Department. At that time, Styrene foremen were salaried.

They organized with about 20 salaried people and the members were each allowed to invite two couples to a party. The first party was planned at the Freeport Community House at Christmas time. As time went on, the beach parties faded from the picture, but the gala Christmas parties became one of the highlights of the social season.

The parties were outstanding for their decorations. One time they completely covered all the walls at the Community House with black paper. Grace Keselik painted stark white fantasy scenes on the black walls. Karol Boundy made three beautiful chandeliers which hung from the ceiling. They were hollow styrofoam chandeliers complete with electric lights.

Many of the parties were costume affairs, and the participants went all out to have the best and most unique costumes. For one party, Margaret Davenport was the costume winner with a Turk's tunic and pantaloons. John Keselik was an alchemist with Spanish moss for whiskers and cabal-covered pointed hat. At one party, Dr. J. A. Stewart came dressed as a white bunny with long white ears and a cottontail.

The Paul Shelleys were an outstanding couple at one party, representing a saint and a sinner. Paul had a styrofoam halo which was lighted, and he wore a white robe embroidered in gold. Marjorie was a sinner, wearing a tight black satin skirt with a slit up one side. She also wore black lace stockings and high heels.

There was always a live band for the dances. Everyone brought their own bottles, and refreshments were served at the dance, including turkey, ham, cold cuts, etc. Some of the parties were catered by the Dow Hotel, and Mrs. J. E. Walston of Freeport also catered some.

A lot of hard work went into putting on the parties, and everything was done by the Styrene group. Invitations to these parties were probably more sought after than for any other parties of that time. It was like getting an invitation to an inaugural ball.

After many glittering social events, the last Styrene party was held in the late '50s, and the STFSAA organization was disbanded.

*

A hurricane closed the Texas Division August 25-28, 1945. New products that year were Ethylene Oxide, Magnesium

EASTER BUNNY?—
No, it's really Dr. J. A. Stewart and wife Marge, fitted out for one of the Styrene costume parties.

AT RIGHT:
Grace Keselik was artistic even then, as proven by this stark white fantasy she sketched.

Anodes, Methyl Chloroform, Propylene Glycol, Tetraethylene Glycol, and Vinylidene Chloride.

V. E. Day was May 8, 1945. The atomic bomb was dropped on Hiroshima on August 6, 1945. On August 9, 1945, the atomic bomb was dropped on Nagasaki. August 10, 1945, was V. J. Day, and there was big celebrating that night. Some reported for work the next morning only to be sent home for a two-day holiday. Others celebrated right through from the 10th till the morning of the 12th.

V. J. Day meant getting back to a 40-hour work week, getting off work at 4:30 p.m., and lifting of most rationing—including gasoline. Everyone who could, gassed up the old car and went for a long trip.

THE WAR WAS OVER!

29

Softball Brought
Lake Jackson National Fame

ON WEDNESDAY, March 27, 1946, the Lake Jackson businessmen decided to sponsor a softball team. The team was called the Lake Jackson Allstars. In 1947, the name was changed to the Lake Jackson Gators. They were the Texas State Champions in 1946, 1950, 1951, 1953, 1955 and 1956. In 1953 and 1956, they won the Southwest Regional Tournaments. They went to Miami in 1953, and to Sacramento in 1956 to the World Tournament.

Speedy Bullard, ace catcher and longtime manager of the team, remembers how it started. Speedy had a fascinating history of the sport himself. He came from Center, in East Texas, where he started playing softball and baseball in vacant lots at the age of 14. Later, he spent three years in the Tenth Air Force with General Claire Chenault's Flying Tigers, playing softball in Australia, India, China, and Burma. On return to this country, Speedy played with the powerful Ellington Field team, which won the State Softball Title and Texas Air Force Championship in 1944.

After getting out of the service, Speedy ran into Gene Faull (whom he had met in Burma), Herschel Orr and Rube Tracy in Lake Jackson. There were several softball teams in the Dow departments, and they decided to take the best players from each team and form the Lake Jackson team. They won the state title in 1946 by beating the Houston Slush Pump team at the state meet in Houston.

Art Webb was named vice president of the Texas Softball Association in charge of Zone Six, which included five softball districts. Jimmy Carroll, also of Lake Jackson, was named commissioner of District 22, which comprised nine counties, including Brazoria County.

In 1947, Billy Graham, first baseman, and Bobby Reed, third baseman, joined the team. Billy Moore came from Alabama about the same time. He was one of the better athletes of the day. Softball beat baseball out of a major leaguer when Moore came to softball.

The team had top pitchers. Besides Gene Faull, there was Hayden Leus, and later, Clayton Dugger, who came from the Waco Outlaw League, which had itself won a World Tournament. Then Weldon Haney came from Dallas. Another great pitcher was Ross Vick. He was only 19 years old, and they had to get him to sign a minor's release to play in the tournament.

Speedy and Jim Scherdin were known as "The Piston." They scouted out Vick, and later on, Harvey Whitehead from

THE GATORS

Galveston. He was one of the best athletes Speedy ever knew. Red Manross was a great hitter, a great athlete, and a great clown, entertaining one and all at the games.

The strangest game Speedy ever played in was with Hiway Inn of Harlingen on July 5, 1947, in Lake Jackson. The game went 26 innings before the Gators won 1-0, and pitcher Gene Faull landed in RIPLEY'S BELIEVE IT OR NOT column with 49 strikeouts. Speedy, the catcher, had 52 other put outs, which is probably a record for one game.

Gene Faull was named the "World's Strikeout King" by the American Softball Association which is made up of 750,000 softball teams. They gave Gene a special trophy in commemoration.

In 1953, the world softball defending champions, the Dow A. C. Team of Midland, Michigan, came to Lake Jackson to play the Gators a five-game tournament. Lake Jackson beat the defending champs three out of five games. It was said the tournament brought the largest crowds ever gathered in Lake Jackson up to that time.

During these exciting years of winning state championships, the Gators felt they were the ambassadors for the city of Lake Jackson all over the state and beyond, where they helped people to know about the new city in Texas.

Dow was a great supporter of the team, and most of the members were Dow employees. They told everyone about the Dow Chemical Co. wherever they went. While at the World Tournament in Sacramento, California, in 1956, the Dow people came up from the Pittsburgh plant and showed the team a wonderful time, taking them wherever they wanted to go in personal cars.

The players had an agreement that when they couldn't beat the best, they would quit. They were state champions in 1956, and so they went direct to the Regional Tournament in 1957. They went on to the semifinals, where Houston beat them in 13 innings. They couldn't beat the best, so that was the end of the old Gator team.

*

In June of 1945, five Dow Texas Division women employees were picked from Plant A to represent their departments in the

Lake Jackson Jaycee Fourth of July Beauty Contest. This was part of the national Miss America Contest. The five contestants were Gene Phillips, Betty Ruth Houston, Doris Grubbs, Mildred Waller, and Joyce Leggett. However, the local contest was won by an employee from Plant B, Betty Ansley. She also went on to win fourth place in the Miss Texas Contest.

INDUSTRIAL PULCHRITUDE

30

Lake Jackson Bank Opened In Tiny Triangle

NEWCOMER ERNIE Rea was in Rube Tracey's hardware store in Lake Jackson when he asked directions to get to 222 Camellia. Three different people tried to tell him, each with a different version. Finally, one said, "Come on, I'll get my car and lead you. I can't tell you." Thus Ernie found the house which he later bought. He'd been very impressed with the friendliness and helpfulness of the Lake Jackson people to a stranger.

In early 1947, Ernie was looking for a location for a business. Downtown Lake Jackson looked a lot different then. Some old Camp Chemical barracks had been moved to a site across North Parking Way from the theater. Only half of the street had been paved. The buildings actually sat on the west half of the street right-of-way. A few businesses were still using these buildings.

The only building north of the theater was Farrell's grocery store, where you could charge your groceries on a tab until payday. You could also call in your order and Farrell's would package it up and deliver it to your home.

Down on This Way was located Burley Schmidt's gas station, the Lake Drug Store, the Piggly Wiggly, the Federated Store, and the Ben Franklin Variety Store. Thick woods grew across the street to the north, but the street was paved double width from the gas station to the end of the Ben Franklin Store. Across Parking Way was all woods.

The road to Brazoria had not yet been built. The only other building was the Dow office building row, housing the Lake Jackson Department, A. C. Ray's real estate firm, Ivan Greer's housing firm, the post office, a beauty parlor, Tom Vaughan's barber shop, City Hall, Dr. R. C. Miller's office, and the telephone office.

A few weeks later when Ernie came to stay and take over the Ben Franklin Store, the old barracks buildings had been moved around to a location across the street from Piggly Wiggly to make room for paving the other half of the street, beside the theater. The barracks buildings housed Pop Hamrick's Lariat Book Store, Gus and Frances Lindveit's *Lake Jackson News* office, Rube Tracey's hardware store (he had previously bought it from Bowen and Ohlrogge), Julia May's LaVelle Shop, Wilson Dowell's Jewelry, Cuz Lee's appliance repair shop, and the one and only Lake Jackson Cafe, owned by Les May and Jimmy Hardis.

The Lake Jackson Bank had just been opened in a little triangular room, in the back of the Piggly Wiggly store, which had been designed as an incinerator for the grocery store. No other place could be found at the time. It was so small there was just one chair and a desk in the lobby for the loan officer, so you had to whisper as you asked for a loan or all of the employees and other bank customers would hear. Art Webb was president, and Bill Parkes was the bank's executive vice president.

Jimmy Carroll was here still earlier. He and L. C. Morrison bought the three-month-old grocery store in 1943, and made it a Piggly Wiggly franchise store. He remembered the problems of wartime rationing. He received his allotment of cigarettes once a week and, in order to be fair, he would only sell one pack to a customer as long as they lasted. The line was so long he couldn't check out any groceries while the cigarettes were being sold. He finally had to move a cash register on a portable table to the doorway on the south side of the store, just to handle the cigarette sales.

After the war was over, Jimmy once visited a neighbor who

showed him drawer after drawer filled with packages of cigarettes. They were so old they were dried and full of worms. The neighbor said she didn't smoke, but during the war when cigarettes were rationed, she bought every package she could get.

Carroll also remembered the 1945 hurricane. The next day when the storm was over, there was no fresh milk in town. Gus Lindveit, who kept a cow in back of his home on Winding Way, furnished fresh milk for a few days to the families with babies.

GRAND OPENING—Buster Curry was the first customer when Lake Jackson's first bank opened its doors. In this photo loaned by The Brazorian News, bank executive vice president Bill Parkes watches the initial business transaction from behind Curry.

Raymond Hinkle remembers Tom Vaughn's barber shop where he worked as a part-time barber. Tom had opened his barber shop in 1943 with four chairs—the first and only barber shop in town for a long time. Tom had moved to Lake Jackson from Cameron, Texas, where he also had a barber shop. He closed it and moved to Lake Jackson, because he heard there was big money to be made.

Tom was loved by all in Lake Jackson, and he was known as a fast hair cutter. He trimmed short and cut high. He was strong on the clippers and didn't waste much time with the shears. One day when the shop was full of customers, a stranger came in. When it came his turn, he got in the chair and Tom was through with him in about five minutes. The stranger asked Tom, "What army post did you work in?"

Back in those days, a haircut was $1, and a shave was 50¢.

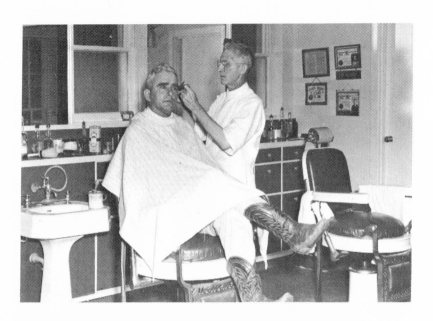

REMEMBERING —Early Lake Jackson, businesses included Tom Vaughan's barbershop, shown as the proprietor gives the new city's first marshal and chief of police, J. S. "Cap" Brown a haircut. The city's first bank, initially chartered as The Lake Jackson State Bank, was housed in a small triangular building designed as an incinerator for the grocery store which is now the TAC office building.

31

Hurricane Club Was 'In' Place

DOES ANYONE remember the Hurricane Club? I remember one night there. People shivered slightly in their seats in the darkened room as the lights flickered shakily, the thunder roared, and the sound of a drenching hurricane rainstorm sounded overhead. A dimly lit scene showed trees bending before hurricane winds. Loose branches, scraps of lumber and debris seemed to move across the field of vision, reminding one all too well of a terrifying Gulf Coast hurricane.

Andy Castorino had just produced his mock "Hurricane" for the customers at Castor's famous Hurricane Club on Highway 288 in Clute.

Andy had first become known when he ran The Oaks on Highway 36 between Freeport and Brazoria. However, in 1946, he decided to move with the people, so he built a small wooden tavern on the new Highway 288 at Clute. He called it the Cozy Nook. It wasn't long before he built a brick building alongside to serve meals.

In 1948, Andy cleared away the Cozy Nook, and on the same spot built his famous Hurricane Club, where he served food, beer and setups. The club also had a dance hall where live bands played each Friday and Saturday night.

For the big opening night of Andy's Hurricane Club, he brought down Buddy Brock's big band from Houston. To add to the festivity, he hung a big mirrored ball from the ceiling which turned while a spotlight played on it, reflecting the light onto the dancers.

Andy's special feature of the club, however, was his man-made hurricane production. There was a big mural painted on one wall showing a tropical scene of mountains, valley, trees, animals, and a river, which under the flickering lights and flashes of lightning, gave the appearance of the place enduring a tropical hurricane. He used a recording of thunder and built up the sound with an amplifier. To simulate the rainstorm, he used a big sheet of iron with a flood of water forced against it. Andy had been a Dow engineer, and he went all out to produce his hurricane.

Andy served a good steak and shrimp cocktail, along with his famous wop salad, french fries, hot garlic bread and plenty of cold beer. The combination was hard to beat.

As good as his other food was, Andy's wop salad was the finest thing on the menu. According to many seasoned travelers, it has never been equaled in this area, or anywhere else in the country. Castorino's brother-in-law, Andy Vargosko, worked at the Hurricane Club for several years and knew the ingredients put in the salad. Vargosko said he had tried many times to reproduce the salad, but simply could not make it taste and smell the way Castorino could.

The dance hall was busy nightly with Dow department parties, firemen's balls, civic club parties, etc. There was a stage in the hall, and many parties engaged their own bands.

The county was dry as far as hard liquor was concerned, but Andy furnished setups and pitchers of ice, and, of course, there was lots of ice cold beer. Customers always enjoyed the personal company of Andy and Mary Castorino, who seemed like good neighbors and friends to all.

Andy closed the Hurricane Club in 1957, ending an interesting entertainment era.

*

Jack Giesecke, who took over as editor of the *DOW TEXAN* in September 1946, will be remembered as the creator of the whimsical character, "Skeebo." This character made periodic letter reports in the *DOW TEXAN* covering events and happenings in the Texas Division, using colorful backwoods language.

In October of 1946, The Dow Texas Division bought its own eight-passenger airplane, a Beechcraft D-18-S, which could cruise over 1,000 miles at a speed of 200 miles per hour. The pilot was H. E. "Ted" Merchant, and the mechanic was C. W. Richards. The plane was based in Houston at Hobby Field for a time, until an airport was built at Lake Jackson and the Division airplane operations were then headquartered down here.

Also in October 1946, Dow bid on the government-owned plants in Freeport. The bid on the government-owned facilities at Plant A was accepted and it was sold to Dow for $1,498,743.

The following January of 1947, all of Plant B, except the magnesium production units, the Styrene plant and the Thiokol plant, were bought by Dow for $35 million. Dr. Dow said this was the largest check Dow had ever written.

New Dow products in 1946 were Ethylene Chloride, Ethylidene Chloride, Sodium Ortho Silicate, Synthetic Magnesite, and Vinyl Chloride.

In the late '40s, a square dance club known as the Flying F got started in Brazosport. Dick Preston and E. Jack Turner were members, and both were callers for the club. Viola Preston tells that the club met monthly to square dance, but in between the regular meetings, members danced in homes and with other clubs as many as three times a week.

DOW TEXAS DIVISION'S BEECHCRAFT

FLYING F MEMBERS—Four members of the Flying F
Dance Club are shown between dances. From left, E.
Jack Turner, then president; Elaine Newcomb, Dorothy
Breeding, and Dick Preston. The 40 to 50 members
represented a good cross section of the community.

32

Ever Hear of The Oakdale Plunge?

NOW LET me briefly review some of the events that were taking place in and around the Dow Texas Division in 1947 and 1948.

In April of 1947, Dow Texas Division personnel lent a hand at the terrible Texas City disaster when the French freighter, S. S. *Grandchamp*, exploded leaving 800 missing or dead, in addition to 3,000 injured in the Texas City area.

Also that year, a story was put out on Dow's water transportation facilities. At the start of the war, Benzol was shipped into the Styrene plant by barge from Pittsburgh, Chicago, and other points. Then, out-bound Styrene was shipped by barge in 1946. Rubber-lined acid barges carrying two million pounds of chemicals were the largest of their kind in the U. S. Many went to a barge terminal on the Ohio River at Cincinnati. It took one month for a round trip of 3,700 miles to Cincinnati.

New products in 1947 were Methyl Chloride and Trichlorethylene.

In October of 1947, the plant cafeterias instituted meatless Tuesdays and Thursdays without poultry. This was done to save grain for President Truman's voluntary program to provide food for Europe. The cafeterias saved 100 pounds of meat and 10 dozen eggs a week.

The same year, Dow Mag Hospital was bought from the government by Dow, and was increased from 42 beds to 74 beds.

Early in 1948, radar equipment became available and was installed at Plant A for hurricane detection. A powerful radar set, weighing five tons and containing 150 vacuum tubes, was installed in a hurricane-proof building. It had a big, saucer-shaped, eight-foot antenna, and was placed on the river levee to the right of the Surfside Beach road at the barge canal bridge. The radar started its watchdog duties, and all the data obtained was channeled direct to the Weather Bureau for analysis.

In January of 1948, the Stratton Ridge facilities were ready for operation. In the spring, Ethylene II began operation, and in Plant B, Chlorine III started up. Glycol II followed.

*

Late in 1948, the City of Lake Jackson decided to build the first municipal swimming pool in the area. The city had voted $4,000 in park bonds, and it was decided to use it all for a swimming pool. The municipal pool was to be located on Magnolia, between Center Way and Winding Way.

Bob Graves, a Dow engineer, offered to furnish the engineering and construction supervision free. Many contractors also offered to help with labor and material at or below cost. It took a real community effort to get a full-size municipal pool built for $4,000, but somehow it was done, and about 99 percent of the Lake Jackson populace turned out for the opening in June of 1949.

Someone had a great idea to run a contest to name the new swimming pool, and lots of names were turned in. It was finally decided the winning name would be "Oakdale Plunge," which seemed a fitting name for the new recreational facility amid the oak trees. Somehow, the name never caught on, and I'll bet there are only a very few of you who remember it as "Oakdale Plunge."

*

I must tell you of an episode in late 1949 or early 1950, involving Dow's Levi Leathers. A. J. Keesee, of the fire department at Dow Plant A, tells about it.

It seems that the new V1V2 plant was giving some trouble in its operation, and a lot of effort was being made to get it straightened out. One night after midnight, Keesee was making his rounds at V1V2 when in came Dow executive Levi Leathers in his robe. Levi had thought of a solution while in bed, so he got up, put on a robe, and came down to the plant. Levi looked over the situation and put his idea to work, which solved the problem. This is an example of how Dow people got the job done.

By the way, I have heard it said by knowledgeable people in Dow that Levi Leathers is one of the top chemical process engineers in the whole world.

THE OAKDALE PLUNGE—Mayor Bill Colegrove turns the first spade of dirt to start construction on the first municipal swimming pool in Brazosport. Although the pool has remained a popular spot over the years, probably few of the thousands who have enjoyed leisure hours and learned to swim there ever knew it by its formal name.

33

River Inn Famous For Root Beer and Ice Cream

"OPPRESSIVE, HOT, humid air engulfed the interior of the root beer stand, coming in through its two open-air sides above the counter tops.

"The root beer stand was an old-fashioned drive-in, but the car hops were long since gone. The root beer was still served in heavy frosted mugs and the ice cream was hand packed Lady Borden's.

"Henry Antonelli sat on a stool behind the front counter fanning himself with a section of the evening paper and watched the cars go by."

This is the way Carolyn Luke Reding remembers her Uncle Henry when the famous root beer stand was open in the summer.

Antonelli had opened the stand, called the River Inn, on West Second Street in Freeport about 1923. It had brightly colored gingerbread awnings and outdoor picnic tables and benches. He started with 10-cent hamburgers, and ice cream was five cents a dip. Soon after he opened, he got his root beer keg and started making his own root beer, which he sold at five cents for a large mug.

During the '40s and '50s, this was a favorite watering place for lots of Dow families because of the quality of food and drink Antonelli dispensed. He mixed his own root beer and cooled it down until it was icy cold. When he drew it for a customer, he always had a big heavy frosted mug ready to hold the root beer. No ice went in the mug—what you got was cold, delicious root beer in an icy glass, without the drink being diluted by melting ice.

Antonelli would draw the mug full of root beer and the foam would rise up and flow over the glass. He would wait till the foam was gone and then continue to fill the mug to the brim.

The ice cream might be a big double dip buttered pecan cone using nothing but Lady Borden ice cream. If you bought some to take home, it was Lady Borden tightly hand packed. Antonelli said that Lady Borden was the best ice cream you could buy, and that was all he would serve. His hamburgers and other snacks were of the same high quality.

On the west side of the strand was a lone rare pecan tree giving some shade to that side. It was hard to match the feeling of savoring a cold root beer while sitting on a bench under the tree.

During watermelon season, Antonelli would put up a tarp for more shade and protection from occasional showers, and chill watermelons in big barrels. They were crisply cold when you bought them.

In the summer of 1979, Antonelli closed the River Inn after serving the greatest root beer and ice cream every spring, summer and fall for 56 years. Over the years, the River Inn has been the subject for many artists, and also several articles have been written about it. Some of the foregoing information is from previous "Facts" articles.

*

The tragic death of Willard Dow in 1949 was a terrible blow to all who knew him. He was chairman of the board, president, and general manager of the Dow Chemical Co., and his death in an airplane crash on March 31, 1949, at London, Ontario, sent a shock wave through the whole company.

During the war, Dow operated its own magnesium plant at Freeport, while at the same time it was responsible for the government-owned Dow Magnesium Corporation plant at Velasco. A question arose as to the loan of spare equipment from one plant to another in case of equipment failure at either one.

It was Willard Dow who decreed that Dow equipment would be available in an emergency at D. M. C., but in no case was D. M. C. equipment to be loaned to Dow. It was a costly decision from the Dow Chemical Co. standpoint, but a conscientious one which eliminated any possible conflict of interest.

A 1945 GATHERING —Social gatherings of a formal nature were often held in the Dow Hotel Dining Room, site of this 1945 photo of a going away party for the wife of Dow Texas Division safety director Bill Bragg. She's fourth from left in the front row. Can you identify some of the others despite the dress and hair styles of that era?

A COLD ROOT BEER—Antonelli's River Inn became
a Freeport landmark with its bright Neopolitan decor
attracting not only the thirsty but also local painters.
One example is this piece owned by Henry Antonelli's
niece Carolyn Luke Reding.

34

Dow Launched
Tanker Ship In 1949

IN MARCH of 1949, Dow signed a contract to purchase its first tanker ship, the *Marine Chemist*. It docked at Plant A in October where a big open house was held. The same month it left Dow with its first load of chemicals.

The *Marine Chemist* was a 12,500-ton tanker in service from Freeport to the East Coast, Havana, Tampico, Holland and Germany, as well as the West Coast of the U. S. The ship was an oil tanker converted to carry dry and liquid chemicals. It had double bulkheads to ensure isolation of each section of cargo from other cargos and from seawater, to maintain the high degree of product purity required.

Separate transfer systems of pipes, connectors, and vents for each different product were provided. This enabled the ship to load and discharge all sections of a varied cargo simultaneously without contamination of any product.

*

The Texas Division was shut down by a hurricane in October of 1949. A final shutdown notice was given on a Monday at 4 p.m. The hurricane harassed Freeport from 10-11 p.m. that night, and then moved on through Houston. The "all clear" was given to return to Freeport at 6 a.m. on Tuesday. By an all-out effort, most plants were in operation that night.

No new plants or products evolved in 1949.

*

By the mid '40s, the Dow Community Band had come into existence. I asked Bob Winston, trumpet player, third from the right in the front row of the adjacent rehearsal picture, about what year the picture was taken. He told me it must have been 1944 if he was in the trumpet section. He remembers he had an accident in the fall of 1944 and broke several front teeth. Thereafter he was forced to play the "peck horn" in the back row.

*

In 1950, a new expansion was under way in both Plants A and B. The ammonia plant was built and the latex plant went on stream. Another new plant was trichloroethylene. By October, the first car of ammonia was shipped.

The government returned the DMC 243 Magnesium production facilities to operation in 1951, and leased the plant to Dow, in order to supply 160 million pounds per year of metal to the government.

The first 10-year service pins for the Texas Division were presented in November, 1951. There were 351 employees eligible which included only one woman, Mildred Schaer.

New plants that year were Chlorine 4, Glycol 3, Light Hydrocarbon 3 and 4, and Polyglycols.

The 100-voice Dow male chorus from Midland, Michigan, came to Texas in March and presented a concert which was well attended and thoroughly enjoyed by the Texas folks.

During May of 1952, Dr. W. R. Veazey, chairman of the Corporate Committee for Research, took a magnesium spade and broke ground for the new W. R. Veazey Research Center. C. M. Shigley, then director of technical research, tells a story of Dr. Veazey during the time plans for the new research center were being developed.

TAKE FIVE—The Dow Community Band played at civic functions and gave concerts at Christmas and in outdoor locations in summer. T. J. Dunbar Jr., for whom Dunbar Park is named, is seen at extreme right in the front row.

Dr. Veazey told Earle Barnes, then director of organic research in Texas, and Shigley, that he would approve the new research center plans under one condition—there must be one room in the administrative offices equipped with a desk, a chair, and a sofa, but no telephone, to which Barnes or Shigley could go and be alone with his thoughts, if he wanted to. Such a room was provided and used as Dr. Veazey suggested. Sadly, Dr. Veazey was unable to attend the dedication of the W. R. Veazey Research Center, and he died without seeing it.

In 1952, Chives Evans of the Chemical Engineering Department got a patent on Sea Salt. It was dehydrated seawater with all of the dissolved minerals in seawater including the trace elements. Evans had developed and patented a way to do it, giving a dry free-flowing salt mixture.

There were many (but unscientifically supported) testimonials about its merits. Among these merits were said to be the relief of arthritis, reduced dental caries, better protection against heat exhaustion, increased potency, and increased fertility. Later, labeling and interstate shipping restrictions by the Federal Drug Administration brought an end to Dow's part in the production of Sea Salt.

The fall of 1952 saw the Ethyl Dow expansion completed, bringing the production of bromine from seawater to 300,000 pounds per day.

THE MARINE CHEMIST—The first Dow-owned tanker ship is shown at dock in Freeport. It was purchased in 1949.

35

"Shooting Stars"
Was Popular Spoof

IN THE early '50s, the Lake Jackson Jaycees presented a large cast of Jaycees in the exciting musical entitled *Shooting Stars*. It was performed by an all male cast on the stage of the Lake Jackson Junior High Cafetorium, with Sally Ross as the pianist. The accompanying picture gives you an idea of the players and the costumes, which added a great deal to the show.

The setting for the show was in a television studio. The playbill lists a number of acts and the Jaycees who starred in them.

The Dancing Darlings were Bob Harrell, Ray Ledlie, John Gentry, Herman Musgrove, John Savaso, John Myers, Bob Scantlin, Vance Smith, Stan Ross, "Stinky" Davis, J. P. Dansby, and Mayor Bill Colegrove.

Red Skelton was played by Joe Musgrove.

The Bubbles Dancers included Fred Schneider, Earl Compton, and Jerry McIntire.

In "At the Age of Three," Eleanor Roosevelt was played by "Stinky" Davis; Dagmar by Jim Hiner; and Faye Emerson by Bob Franklin.

The Roxy Rockettes, "Beautiful of Face and Figure," were

HOW MANY OF THE *SHOOTING STARS* IN THIS GALAXY FROM THE PAST CAN YOU IDENTIFY?

Bob Scantlin, Stan Ross, Vance Smith, Bill Colegrove, and "Stinky" Davis.

Needless to say, everyone had a good time—the audience as well as the players.

*

Harold Nelson opened a little place at the junction of Highways 332 and 288 in July 1952. He wanted a catchy name for the store and decided on Bodiddle's. It was indeed catchy— just about every person who drove by and saw the sign never forgot it.

The store started out small, in a little building two garage doors wide. Each morning Nelson would roll up the garage doors and push out racks containing bread, candy, and a checkout counter, and start selling. The building was all open to the front and had only a roof and three sides. At night he simply rolled all the racks back inside, pulled down the garage doors and closed.

After a time, Nelson added a storeroom and later a covered patio, as the money became available. "I like to starved to death trying to improve that place," Nelson said. His next addition was a barbeque area with a pit and serving counter.

Soon thereafter came Hurricane Carla. Bodiddle's was so far under water, it was one of several buildings pictured in a brochure to inform the governor of Texas how bad the hurricane destruction was to local businesses. It didn't discourage Nelson though. He and his wife cleaned up and rebuilt the store, enlarging it considerably and closing everything in. He built another bar and made the area behind the barbeque pit into an attractive patio lounge area with a neat fence around it. Umbrella tables were also used to add charm.

After Nelson rebuilt Bodiddle's, the bar and barbeque were open till midnight on weeknights and till 1 a.m. on Saturday, but the grocery and sporting goods store never closed. They didn't even have locks on the doors. Nelson couldn't believe the number of people moving around at night. There were many shift workers who got off at midnight and weren't quite ready to go to bed, as well as many hunters and fishermen who came by early in the morning to get licenses, equipment, lunch items, etc.

I asked Nelson if there were many fights in his place. He said, "No, we catered to lovers, not fighters." He would ask someone to leave if he saw them leaning toward trouble. Sometimes these were our "better" citizens, and sometimes not-so-good citizens.

The place, particularly the outdoor patio area, was really a nice workingmen's club—clean and not too fancy—catering to people coming or going to work, as well as families who brought their children. I used to go by for some of Nelson's great barbeque. Several judges and attorneys would come down from the courthouse in Angleton, too. Nelson said I was a coat and tie

BODIDDLE'S HAD 15 DEPARTMENTS–JUST COUNT 'EM.

man, and while he was glad to see me, he really catered to the working men.

Banker Fred Palmer said Bodiddle's cashed more checks than the local banks. Sometimes the check cashing line would be 200 feet long. Cars would be parked along the road almost to the intersection.

A highlight Nelson said he won't forget is the one and only time Dr. A. P. Beutel, Dow Texas Division's general manager, paid a visit when he still had the old Bodiddle's. Nelson was sweeping one morning when Dr. Beutel came in and said, "I have been hearing all kinds of reports about Bodiddle's, and I wanted to come by and see what you have." Nelson still speaks of what a good neighbor Dow was to him.

On Sunday, December 3, 1967, Bodiddle's Barbeque, Beer, Groceries, Fishing Tackle, and Boat Store closed forever to make way for the new multi-level interchange for Highways 332 and 288. The last two days Nelson served free beer. "I had to get rid of the keg beer," Nelson said.

36

Imbibers Club
Outlasted Its Bylaws

THE TEXAS Division opened the following new plants in 1952: Butadiene, Caustic Evaporators 2, Chlorine 5, Magnesium Alloy, and Perchloroethylene 2. That year water shipment of chemicals became more important to Dow Texas when the first shipment of Styrene was made on the *Marine Chemist*. This was followed by the first shipments of caustic to Cuba in 1953.

The seawater intake at Plant A was taken over by an army of jellyfish in 1953, and nearly stopped the seawater supply.

In April of that year, the keel was laid for Dow's second seawater ship, the *Marine Dow Chem*. The tanker was launched in December, and first arrived in Freeport in April of 1954. The 17,000-ton tanker was the first ship designed and built specifically for transporting liquid chemicals. It was built for lease to Dow and was the world's largest vessel for chemical service, with the capacity to handle 11 different kinds of chemicals at the same time.

The ship carried basic chemicals, including 50 percent and 73 percent caustic soda. One of its features was the nickel-clad heated cargo tanks for the 73 percent caustic soda, which no one

161

had ever attempted to ship in bulk by water. Specially designed lines and pumps through which this caustic would pass were also of nickel. About 100,000 pounds of pure nickel went into these facilities.

Another engineering first in the tanker was cathodic protection against hull erosion. Magnesium anodes weighing 60 pounds each were bolted to the sides of the ship—forward, amidships, and aft. This enabled Dow to ship more chemicals farther from the Texas Division, and at less cost, than ever before.

*

One day in 1953, Henry Litchfield, Jim Crews, Jack Waltrip, and Jack Reid had stopped at Axel's beer hall in Clute on the way home from bowling, and were having a little cooling refreshment while playing shuffleboard. Henry put down his beer and said, "Our wives are picking on us all the time because we go out to bowl and drink a little beer without asking them to join us. Let's form a club, meet once a month, and invite the wives."

Everyone liked the idea, and they decided to organize the club. They would meet at the Dow Lake Jackson Pavilion, have a steak dinner, and plenty of keg beer. Since the wives would be invited, Reid said that to belong you would have to like girls and like beer.

Litchfield thought the club should be named the "Liars Club," but he was outvoted. The name "Nippers and Imbibers Society" was chosen because it was descriptive and had a certain elegance.

Reid and Litchfield put on the first party. The four oganizers invited some friends and there were about 18 to 20 people. They served broiled steaks (basted in beer), baked potatoes, a green salad and bread. There were also two kegs of beer. Reid and Litchfield wanted to be sure they had enough.

At the first meeting Crews was elected president, and he agreed to put on the next month's party, even though he thought the election was rigged. Reid said it wasn't, because they had gotten a lot of capsules from the drug store and had written a different name on each one. Crews said his name was on every capsule.

Everyone thought Crews would be president for a year, but at the next meeting when he rose to give his acceptance speech, he produced a set of bylaws written on a napkin. The first bylaw provided that a new president would be elected each month. After a big fight over the bylaws, they were finally accepted as written on the napkin. From time to time thereafter, someone would ask for information on the bylaws, but no one could find the napkin.

The format for the parties was quite simple. The president was in complete charge of buying the steaks, beer and other food, as well as seeing to all the preparation. The meetings were called for 6:30 p.m., and everyone would sit around and visit, sipping cold suds, until about 8 p.m., or whenever the steaks were ready. After the enjoyable dinner, an election would be held for a new president. This always caused a lot of conversation and arguing. If elected, you had to take the job or get out of the club.

After the election, the president would total up the costs and divide the amount among the couples present. Anyone who didn't pay their share by the next day would have his name posted on the bulletin board at the Lake Drug Store. The final item on the agenda was to finish off the keg of beer.

A number of new members were invited in order to have enough manpower to fill the new president's job each month. Soon the club had about 20 to 25 couples. The club ran for three or four years, until one of the presidents had to be out of town on the meeting night, which meant postponement. Shortly thereafter the club disbanded.

The meetings had been friendly, pleasant social gatherings with a simple program—visit, sip beer, eat a steak dinner, elect a new president, and finish the keg. The total cost would be $4 to $5 a couple. I still remember someone bringing up something from the bylaws and everyone would yell, "Crews, where is the napkin?"

STILL ARGUING?
—It's likely that the topic of conversation between Jim Crews, left, and Jack Reid might be the controversial by-laws of a long-disbanded club which used to meet in the Dow Pavilion by which they are standing.

SECOND TANKER—The Marine Dow Chem was the second seawater ship purchased for use by the Dow Texas Division. This shows her in 1954.

37

Adding Plane
Cut Dow Travel Time

IN 1950, Dow put into operation a DC-3 airplane in the Texas Division. It was an Army C-47 plane which had been converted to an executive airplane configuration with 13 seats. The plane was used a great deal to fly Texas Dow people to and from the Dow headquarters in Midland, Michigan. Normally the number of passengers on these flights was restricted to eight, in order to provide more comfort and to avoid stops for refueling.

The flight took some seven hours each way. Usually the plane would leave Sunday morning taking passengers to Midland, and return them to Texas on Wednesday or Thursday. This would give the Dow people two or three days to do their work in Michigan.

Ted Merchant was the chief pilot and in charge of airplane operations for Texas. For a short time, the plane operated out of Hobby Airport in Houston, but later moved to Lake Jackson when the airport was built there.

Flying between Michigan and Texas was a far cry from the old train connections we had once used. To come to Texas by train, we would first drive 22 miles from Midland to the Saginaw depot of the Michigan Central Railroad and board a sleeper on

165

DOW TEXAS DIVISION'S DC-3

the siding. At 10:45 p.m. the Michigan Central passenger train would come through from Bay City, pick up the sleeper and take it on down to Jackson, Michigan, where the car would be shunted onto a siding about 1 a.m. After a short time, the New York Central passenger train on the New York to Chicago run would come along and pick up the sleeper.

About breakfast time the next morning, the train would be rounding the south end of Lake Michigan, and would arrive at the Illinois Central depot in Chicago about 8 a.m. There we would pick up our luggage and take a taxi to the Dearborn Street Station to catch the Alton train to St. Louis, which left Chicago about 9 or 10 a.m. After lunch, the train would cross the Mississippi River into the Union Station at St. Louis, arriving about 2 p.m. Mercifully, we didn't have to change stations in St. Louis, but did change trains to the Missouri Pacific Sunshine Special, which departed St. Louis for Houston about 5 p.m.

Dinner would be served in the diner as the train proceeded south. Through the night the train twisted and turned around the southern Missouri and northeastern Arkansas hills, passing through Little Rock and Texarkana, and then down through Longview and Palestine, Texas. As the sun came up, breakfast would be served in the diner while passing through the pretty East Texas pine country. The Sunshine Special would arrive at the Houston Union Station about 11 a.m. Thereafter, it was a two-hour automobile drive to get down to Freeport.

As I said earlier, the seven hours by DC-3 airplane between Michigan and Texas was a far cry from spending 36 to 38 hours on the train for the same trip.

*

In February of 1954, the West Process Area site development started. That was the stretch beyond Chlorine 4, Glycol 3, Light Hydrocarbon 4, and Perchloroethylene 2.

The Brazoria Reservoir was completed in May of 1954. This provided one of the great bass fishing areas of all time in a reservoir which supplied fresh water from the Brazos River for Dow Chemical production.

In late summer, the new bridge over the Intracoastal Canal was scheduled to open. Dow contributed $100,000 to the bridge as a development to help Brazosport's recreational facilities.

*

During January of 1953, the citizens of Lake Jackson decided to celebrate the 10th anniversary of the start of the city. The first residents to move into Lake Jackson had arrived on January 26, 1943. A whole week of activities was planned in commemoration of the anniversary.

On Monday there was a big parade that went not only through the downtown streets of Lake Jackson, but beyond to Clute and Freeport. That night a VIP banquet was held in the Lake Jackson Junior High School cafeteria, with many political and well-known people attending.

Tuesday, Wednesday and Thursday were given over to special events of various kinds put on by churches and civic organizations. Thursday was Plantation Day for all to visit the old plantation site at the lake.

Friday was school day for various activities to celebrate the event. A big street dance was held Saturday night to close the celebration.

WEST PROCESS AREA—In 1954, this was the view from the air of the Dow Texas Division West Process Area in the distance with only Power 4 completed.

38

'50s Brought
New Plants, Products

WHEN GRETCHEN Muehlberg was 10 years old in 1953, her father, Dow's Paul Muehlberg, and mother, Betty, planned a fun birthday party for their daughter. They organized a hayride for Gretchen and her friends by hiring a man with a pair of mules, a wagon and a load of hay. The cost was $10 for the driver, wagon and team, and $5 for the hay.

The driver was David, and he drove the mules and wagon from where the Richwood area is now, all the way to the Muehlberg home on Center Way in Lake Jackson. The hayride went from Gretchen's home, out to Lake Jackson, and then back again to Center Way in Lake Jackson. Gretchen remembers this as one of her best birthday parties.

＊

A Dow landmark was established in 1954 when the Agricultural Research buildings went up at the new site west of the city of Lake Jackson. Dow's Power 3 was also completed that year.

The same year magnesium was first used by Samsonite in a

169

new line of luggage. Magnesium has since become an important material in the manufacture of luggage.

On May 1, 1954, the first Plantation Days celebration was held in Lake Jackson. This marked the 10th anniversary of the incorporation of the city in April of 1944.

*

One morning in July of 1955, Bob Bryant (now a Dow major manager) and his family boarded Eastern Airlines Flight 508 at Hobby Airport in Houston, bound for Idlewild Airport in New York. This was the first step for the Bryant family on their journey to their new home in Rotterdam, the Netherlands. Bob was to be the project manager for the new Botlek Dow terminal and associated light processing units at Rotterdam.

The Dow plan was to include a wholly owned subsidiary in the Netherlands. It would build a manufacturing plant, as well as a tank storage warehouse and dock facilities in Rotterdam. The Bryant family was the first of many Dow Texas Division families to move to Europe and other places around the world.

On July 20, they boarded the Holland American liner, *Nieu Amsterdam*, in New York and sailed to Europe. They had sold their home in Lake Jackson, and took all their belongings, including their car, with them on the ship. In Rotterdam, the Bryants lived in what the Dutch called a *Herren Haus* (or Men's House), but what we call a row house, similar to those in Baltimore.

This move and the Dow construction at Rotterdam was the first of a great Dow European expansion. Later there was the Terneuzen complex in the Netherlands, as well as many other chemical operations in Europe.

*

How many of you remember Levi Cook, Dow's "Shoeshine Boy?" In August of 1955, he was busy shining Dow folks' shoes using a secret cleaner, the name of which he would never divulge. He was probably the only shoeshine boy in the world who had a specially designed and constructed shoeshine box made of magnesium.

*

Dow's first synthetic Glycerine plant went on stream in 1955 with a capacity of 36,000,000 pounds of product per year. This outstanding research and production achievement was under the direction of E. B. Barnes. That year, new Dow products were Polyethylene and Soda Ash, as well as an expansion in the capacity of Ethylene Oxide and Ethylene Glycol.

A story appeared in August 1955 about a new magnesium jet plane for the Air Force. They were testing the F 80-C "Shooting Star," an experimental version of the famed Shooting Star. Being one-third lighter than aluminum, the magnesium could be used in thicker sheets, possessing greater rigidity and permitting a wholesale reduction in the number of rivets and fasteners for the plane—16,000 instead of 42,270.

This left 30 percent more space for fuel than with aluminum, resulting in increased speed and better performance. Additionally, assembly line production of the all-magnesium plane would be 20 percent cheaper than the conventional model.

GRETCHEN'S BIRTHDAY—A birthday hayride was a big event in the life of 10-year-old Gretchen Muehlberg, in 1953. Birthday parties were a big part of the social scene for the younger set.

THE BRYANT FAMILY

39

Big Battle Began Litter-ly In 1957

WHILE ON a trip to Central Europe in 1956, Dr. A. P. Beutel noticed the countrysides and observed how clean and litter free they were. He wondered why we couldn't have the same clean, attractive roadsides and streets in our country.

So in 1957, Beutel asked Dow's Bill Colegrove to organize an effort to at least get Brazoria County cleaned up. That was the beginning of the Keep Brazoria County Beautiful Association, with Mrs. Kate Hayslip of Brazoria as its first president. O. P. "Old Pushbroom" Schnabel, leader of the San Antonio Beautification Association, was a big help in getting our new group organized and moving in the right direction.

County Judge Alton Arnold has served as treasurer for the county organization for over 25 years. Colegrove said, "It would be hard to find anyone better to look after the money than the highly respected County Judge."

Dow cooperated with its full support of the KBCBA. They bought 10,000 litter bags to be distributed to employees, and also furnished cash to pay for a part-time public relations person for the organization. Thelma Willis was the first such PR person.

Many promotional activities and school projects were used to put across the idea of cleanliness. One of the schools held a cleanup cartoon contest, and one of the cartoons was blown up and used on billboards around the county. The amount of trash on the roadways and the cost of removing it was stressed in many ways. As one means of publicizing these facts, a chicken wire enclosure was erected at a busy intersection and all the trash from the nearby roadsides was put in the enclosure. The adjacent photograph, which appeared in a Houston newspaper, shows pretty Barbara Penny Monical emptying trash into the enclosure.

The county organization grew steadily, and along the way encouraged other cities in the county to have their own local clean-up, paint-up, plant-up, and fix-up organizations. An annual prize was given to the city showing the most improvement.

*

Other mid-'50s happenings: A king-size alligator, so large that two lassos were necessary to hold it, was caught in the Dow Plant A waste water canal by W. W. Treat in 1955.

The new Dow airport in Lake Jackson was completed on January 5, 1956. The Dow Cessna airplane landed there that afternoon. The first passenger flight was on January 6, with Dow Texas Division General Manager Dr. A. P. Beutel as passenger.

In February of that year, Dr. Beutel presented a new Brazosport plan of development to the area mayors, city managers, planning commissions, and school and chamber of commerce officials. Beutel said, "Although this study was sponsored by Dow, it is not a Dow plan. We hope it may prove a point of beginning for everyone concerned with community development."

A chief feature of the plan was to coordinate all phases of community growth—residential, educational, recreational, and industrial—into one regional plan. One outstanding feature of the plan was the "Brazosport Loop," a road of expressway size.

*

During May of 1956, the Dow Hotel dining room was remodeled using the exciting new Dow product, Saran, for the carpet. The new carpet and the beautiful wall murals gave a warm, attractive, homey ambiance to this well-liked Dow facility.

That year Dow also donated $20,000 to Freeport to start its section of the new seawall. Additionally, Dow raised and strengthened most of its own levees.

SARAN CARPET IN DOW HOTEL DINING ROOM

CAUTION—Dow's W. F. English, background, and G. R. Smith keep wary eyes on a big 'gator caught near Dow Plant A in 1955.

No new plants were built in 1956, but new products added were Methyl Acetylene and Epichlorhydrin.

After 45 years, the sister cities of Freeport and Velasco, lying on each side of the Brazosport Harbor, were consolidated into one city—Freeport. Although Velasco was the older city, Freeport had grown larger, so the name taken was that of the larger city. However, the historical name Velasco did not totally vanish. It remains in many forms, such as Velasco Drainage District, Velasco Depot on the Missouri Pacific Railroad, etc.

In July of 1957, an important event for the United States and of great interest to the local residents occurred. It was the launching of an earth satellite made of Texas Division Magnesium.

40

Dow Officials
Helped Junior Achievement

DOW TEXAS Division General Manager Dr. A. P. Beutel set up a program for Junior Achievement in Brazosport in June of 1957. At that time the only other Junior Achievement organization in Texas was in Houston. A number of local businessmen met for lunch at the Dow Hotel, and Beutel discussed the need for this program to involve young people in businesses of their own, which would allow them to learn the economic facts of free enterprise.

The group agreed to sponsor six Junior Achievement companies the first year. The late Jack Waltrip, president of the Lake Jackson Bank, was elected president of the group, and Dow's Bill Colegrove was trained as a program director in St. Louis by the National Junior Achievement organization. The local school system made two vacant buildings on the Clute school campus available for the J. A. companies.

High school juniors and seniors were organized into the new J. A. firms. They elected officers, picked out a product to manufacture, and sold stock to finance the company. With the help of adult advisors, they produced the product and went out in the community and sold the product for what they hoped

179

would be a profit. At the end of the school year, the companies were dissolved, and those who had made a profit paid off the stockholders.

It had been an excellent learning experience for this group of young people to find out what it was like to run a business in this country. Since that first year, the program has grown countywide. Junior Achievement has also had remarkable growth nationwide.

*

Dow employees and equipment were used to help flood victims in the wake of flood waters from Oyster Creek and the Brazos River in May of 1957. Dow volunteers worked with the Civil Air Patrol, Red Cross, National Guard, and the Brazosport Boat Club during evacuation and emergency shelter operations, as well as clean-up.

On October 31, 1957, the Plant B Magnesium production facilities were bought from the government for $20,700,000. New plants built that year were Light Hydrocarbon No. 5, Acetylene, Acetylene Hydrochloride, Ethanolamines, Ethylene Diamine, Versenes, and soil fumigants.

New products that year were Monoethanolamines, Diethanolamines, Triethanolamines, Diethylene Triamine, Triethylene Tetramine, Telone, and Dorlone.

The Tourist Promotion Committee of the Brazosport Chamber of Commerce put on a big affair in the summer of 1957. It was Sunfest Days at Surfside Beach, which lasted from Friday, May 31, through Sunday, June 2. It included a bathing beauty contest, fireworks, boxing matches, a water skiing exhibition, and a boat parade and races.

The activities started with a Memorial Day tree planting on the road to Surfside Beach. Possibly a few of you may remember the long row of palm trees planted then. Bob Hammond's Shows, an outstanding carnival, provided entertainment on the beach. Also, strolling troubadors entertained on the beach Friday evening.

A water ski show was held featuring a male skier who held the world's record for kite flying while being towed by a speedboat. The ski show also included flying pyramids, clown acts, and a water ballet by several lovely women.

Boxing matches were held between teams from Brazosport, Angleton and Galveston. Also, marathon boat races, from Freeport to Galveston and back, took place on Saturday. That night a Sand Hop, or Barefoot Beach Dance, was held at Surfside Beach.

The talent portion of the Miss Surfside Beauty Contest was viewed at the Lake Theater in Lake Jackson on Saturday night. At Surfside Beach at 5 p.m. on Sunday, the bathing suit contest finally determined the winner.

Some of the finest boats on the coast were on display in a boat parade in the Intracoastal Canal near Surfside Bridge at 1 p.m. on Sunday. Then at 8 p.m. on Sunday night, the Jax Brewing Company donated a spectacular $2,000 display of fireworks.

Local people working on the various events included Thelma Willis, Tom Reed, Fred Palmer, and Bill Hammonds.

*

The new Administration Center at Plant B, called the A. P. Beutel Building, opened in October of 1957, and many of the executives of the Texas Division moved from the Plant A Administration Building. They had waited a long time. When the Administration Building at A-1201 was built in 1941, it was supposed to be a temporary building for only a few months. It lasted for 16 years.

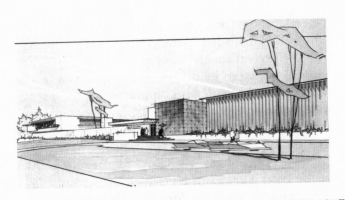

THE A. P. BEUTEL BUILDING, OPENED IN 1957

SUNFEST DAYS—Contestants, from left, Barbara, Penny (Monical), Margo Hanson, and Judy Wannall (Courtright) in the 1957 Miss Surfside Beach contest.

41

United Fund
Proves County Generosity

IN 1958, the Hellgate turbine at Plant B Power House was demolished and removed after 40 years of service at Hellgate Power House, New York, and at Plant B Power.

That year E. J. Lavino announced plans to build a plant at Midway which would produce Periclase, a product used extensively in foundries.

New Dow plants in 1958 were Aluminum Chloride, Glycerine 2, Epoxy Resins, and Power 4.

*

The Brazoria County United Fund received its state charter in June of 1959. Dow's Nelson D. Griswold was the first president of the organization. The old Community Chest had served its purpose, but was limited in the number of agencies it served. Therefore, it was disbanded and the new United Fund (now United Way) was organized. It included many new social agencies such as American Red Cross, a Muscular Dystrophy organization, and others, making it much broader in scope and of a great deal more service to the people of Brazoria County.

The first year's goal of $107,741 was, as in every year since, oversubscribed. The 1982 goal of $1,900,000 was substantially exceeded again, illustrating the continued concern of Brazoria County people.

*

The announcement came from Washington in 1959 that the nation's first Seawater Conservation Plant would be built in Freeport. Dow later donated the land for this plant.

The continued growth of the area was exemplified by the new Dow-Badische plant. This was a joint venture of Dow and the German Badische Company. The plant was dedicated at Freeport in 1959.

New Dow plants in 1959 were Polyethylene, Carbon Monoxide, and Dioxane.

A new editor for the *DOW TEXAN*, Jim Cope, came along in 1960. He began a long association with the Texas Division, progressing to Director of Public Relations before moving on to Dow's regional office in Houston.

During October of 1960, Dow launched another chemical tanker in Massachusetts, the *S. S. Leland I. Doan*, after being christened by Mrs. A. P. Beutel. The tanker was an 18,000-ton deadweight ship, 551 ft. long and 68 ft. wide, with a speed of 18 knots.

A new product in 1960 was magnesium hydroxide, which was a raw material for the new E. J. Lavino plant.

The city of Freeport welcomed the gift of the Freeport Golf Course from Dow, and the city of Lake Jackson was given a downtown Lake Jackson building by Dow for use as a city library.

*

Now I must tell you about a very unusual series of events which took place in 1960. Many of us will never forget them.

On Saturday, July 2, 1960, the city of Lake Jackson, in a surprise move, annexed around both Dow Plants A and B, but left them in protected city-tax-free islands. The city also took in a north corridor between Retrieve Prison Farm and the old Angleton Road, to the point where the road crosses the railroad

CHARTER RECEIVED—Viewing the charter for Brazoria County United Fund are, from left, Sam Lee, Mrs. V. A. Thorpe and Nelson D. Griswold, first president of the organization. United Fund in 1959

track; and a saltgrass area north and east of Freeport—about 15 square miles total. It included the Dow Airport in Lake Jackson and the C.A.P. Airport near Oyster Creek.

Then on Tuesday, July 5, Lake Jackson annexed another 8,000 acres towards Brazoria, between the Brazos River and the Prison Farm, to the railroad bridge just outside of Brazoria. It included Lake Jackson Farms, Riverside Country Club, and other acreage.

Next, on Wednesday evening, July 6, the Freeport City Council annexed a 10-foot strip around everything Lake Jackson had annexed, plus several square miles of acreage through Jones Creek and Brazoria to the San Bernard River, around West Bay and Bastrop Bayou—even 10½ miles out to sea to the tidelands limits.

That same night, July 6, Clute annexed a large slice of territory north toward Angleton, rounding out the "Annexation Circle."

There were wide repercussions in the area. However, the Lake

Jackson Council said it acted on a strong but unidentified tip that more distant cities, presumably Galveston or Texas City, were considering annexation of the Dow plants.

42

Seawater Plant Opened By Kennedy

VICE PRESIDENT Lyndon B. Johnson came to Freeport in June of 1961. The big occasion was the startup of the nation's first Seawater Conversion Plant, located on the old road to Surfside Beach, in the Dow Plant A area. The Conversion Plant was actually started by remote control by President John F. Kennedy from his office in Washington. The President pushed a button on his desk, which by electrical relay turned on the plant in Freeport. Dr. A. P. Beutel and Leland I. Doan, president of Dow, had been invited to Washington by President Kennedy, and were both standing by his desk when he pushed the button.

Following the startup, Vice President Johnson was the guest at a big reception held at the Riverside Country Club. Hundreds of Brazoria County people had the opportunity of seeing him and hearing him discuss the importance of the Seawater Conversion process to all the arid areas of the world.

*

Dr. A. P. Beutel was named outstanding man of the year in 1961 by the Brazosport Chamber of Commerce. The same year, Dow gave its hospital, valued at $1,175,000 to a non-profit association, the Community Hospital of Brazosport.

*

Volumes have been written about the terrible hurricane of 1961 named "Carla," but I believe we should put down here, for posterity, a few comments which will indicate the destruction and the aftermath of such a natural disaster on the Gulf Coast.

C. M. Shigley, assistant general manager in charge of Dow's Technical Research at the time, said Carla was one of the most memorable hurricanes in the Texas Division's experience. It necessitated the evacuation of a large coastal area and did extensive damage to Freeport and to the Dow plants.

Most of the damage was from seawater which either penetrated or circumvented the levees and the plants. Of the eight laboratories in Technical Research, six were invaded by muddy seawater. Porter Hart's Instrument Research Laboratory was under six feet of water. A large Burroughs computer had just been installed in the laboratory, and was irreparably damaged.

In September of 1961, Hurricane Carla hit. The evacuation began on Saturday, September 9. Carla was still in the Gulf and had very high winds on September 10. On Monday, September 11, Carla stopped and began to build up intensity. Freeport levees were leaking and the city was being flooded. Ethyl Dow flume gates were undermined, and all of Plant A was under water. Plant B and the Clute area filled with water due to a low levee at Oyster Creek. On Tuesday, September 12, Carla moved inland at Port O'Connor at 4 a.m., with winds gusting at 150 miles per hour and tides at 13 to 14 feet.

Earle Barnes, in describing the Plant B flooding, said that at 2 p.m. on Monday, Plant B was still dry, Then around noon, what seemed like a tidal wave came in. It moved in from across Highway 288 around the end of the protection levee, and also from the seawater flume in the Brazos River, and was in Plant B by 3:30 p.m. Toward Clute and Oyster Creek, it was just one big bay of water. It was three to four feet deep at Badische, and three to four feet deep in the Styrene parking lot. There was about one foot of water at the east end of Plant B, all around the magnesium area, and flowing out the main gate towards the Ammonia Plant area.

PLANT B FLOODING DURING HURRICANE CARLA

On Wednesday, September 13, repairs were started at the Dow plants. An estimated 20,000 electric motors were under water in the Division. The first problem was to get a foot of water out of east Plant B. Big diesel-driven pumps were needed to evacuate water so Power 2 could be started up. Another problem for the clean-up crews was the absence of drinking water. There was none in the plant, and supplies had to be brought in.

Dow also lent a hand to Brazosport victims. They furnished free two 5,000-gallon tank trucks of Houston drinking water to Freeport and one 5,000-gallon tank truck to Clute. Dow also made 180 rent-free apartments available for 30 days, as well as lending materials for syphons over the outer storm protection levee at Surfside Road.

The American Red Cross also spent $800,000 in the county for shelter operations and rehabilitation of the people who suffered from this terrible storm.

SEAWATER PLANT STARTUP—Dow executives Leland I. Doan and Dr. A. P. Beutel watch as President John F. Kennedy pushes the button to start the Seawater Conversion Plant in Freeport.

43

Lake Jackson
Celebrates Birthday For A Week

DR. A. P. Beutel, general manager of Dow's Texas Division, became vice president of Dow's Gulf Coast operations in October, 1961. E. B. Barnes was named the new general manager of the Texas Division. In 1962, Barnes was awarded an honorary doctorate degree from Texas Christian University.

The Epoxy Novalac semi-plant was completed in 1963. This was the chemical used on the Apollo heat shield for reentering the atmosphere from space.

*

The late Fred Latham was said to be the oldest Jaycee in Texas in the early '60s. He said he had two birth certificates, and it was hard to pin him to a definite age, although he was probably in his 60's then. Latham was an accomplished engineer in Dow's Estimating Department. He had a fertile brain with lots of ideas, all of which he was ready to implement by his own diligent work.

In early 1963, at a meeting of the Lake Jackson Jaycees, Latham stood up and made a suggestion. He thought it was time to recognize the two founders of Lake Jackson—Alden Dow, the architect, and Dr. A. P. Beutel, the farseeing head of the

191

Texas Division, who ramrodded the new city to become a garden spot in the county, and rightly called the "City of Enchantment." Latham suggested that a suitable plaque clad in a magnesium frame and structure be set in the ground under the great oaks in front of Lake Drug where the city was started.

The year 1963 coincided with the 20th anniversary of Lake Jackson, so the Plantation Days celebration was planned for a week to include Founders Day, when the monument would be dedicated.

Latham sold Colonel's commissions at $5 each to finance the celebration, which entitled the holder to a 10 percent discount on any of the celebration events. The Colonel's commissions read:

> "Colonel for the Domain of the Spirits of Lake Jackson," and continued:
>
> "To all spirits of the days of our plantation, wherever ye may be, and to ole Yankees, Cajuns, Michiganders, Tenderfeet, Carpetbaggers, Inhabitants of the Swamp, Texans, Exhausted Roosters, and other of the like ilk.
>
> "Greetings.
>
> "Be it further understood by virtue of the powers vested in us, we do command all money lenders, wine sellers, cabaret owners, Aggies, Teasippers, Ghosts, and all other dwellers in our domain, to show due honor and respect to this good colonel at all times."

The *FACTS* had a 20th Anniversary Edition on Sunday, May 12. The schedule for the anniversary from May 12 to 18 will probably never be duplicated in our lifetime. It included a carnival all week, an art show, king and queen contest, bridge tournament, kids' races, doll buggy parade, southern style meal on Tuesday served by the Lake Jackson Jaycees, softball games, horseshoe tournament, and teenage talent show.

On Wednesday there was a new car display, a Judo exhibition, a golf pitching contest, and a dance show. Thursday brought a boat exhibit, pet show, street dance, and community band concert.

Friday there was a cake walk, kite-flying contest, square dance, pancake supper, showing of a Dow Lake Jackson film, and an Exporters football game. On Saturday, there was a Founders Day parade, fish fry, frog-jumping contest, fiddlers' contest, antique car display, baby picture contest, domino contest, scout skin divers at the Dow Airport, and a costume contest for men and women.

The Founders Day program began at 1 p.m. on Saturday. Dr. A. P. Beutel and Alden Dow were present for the dedication of the monument, and both made remarks. The faces of both men were engraved on the plaque in stainless steel mounted on magnesium plates. The plaque read:

> "The Citizens of Lake Jackson hereby honor A. P. Beutel and Alden B. Dow through whose vision and determination was created this city of enchantment in the heart of a great oak forest of Brazoria County.
>
> 20th Anniversary
>
> 1943 — 1963"

*

For the first time in 1964, Dow Chemical Co. sales passed the billion-dollar mark. That year, at Dr. Barnes' suggestion, the Youth Employment Summer Program for high school and college students was started. Thirty young people were given jobs the first week.

In 1965, Walter Roush was made responsible for 30 technology centers being set up by Dow worldwide, including seven in Texas. Several have said that Walter Roush was perhaps the greatest producer of development people in Dow's history. He had a remarkable talent for bringing young men along where they could move into top development and managerial capacity. The Dow Chemical Co. is heavily staffed with Roush's men.

CELEBRATION—Barbara Monical, and her two daughters, Penny and Tammi, prepare to celebrate Lake Jackson's twentieth anniversary in 1963, during the week of fun, games and entertainment.

44

Carla Truly A Test For General Manager

A HISTORY of Texas Dow during the period of 1940 to 1976 would be incomplete without a few pertinent comments by the living general managers of the Texas Division during those years.

I begin with Dr. Earle B. Barnes, who was general manager of Dow's Texas Division from 1961 until 1966. I talked with him at his home in Jackson, Wyoming, where he had recently bought a cattle ranch, and he was pleased to look back with me to the time when he was general manager.

Barnes had stepped into the job after Dr. A. P. Beutel had held it for 20 years, and had indeed built the Texas Division from scratch with his own firm hand at the helm every day for those 20 years.

Beutel had been made vice president of Gulf Coast operations for Dow, and he had picked Earle Barnes to take over management of the division.

The change struck the whole Texas Division like an earthquake. Barnes had been informed of the change about two weeks before the announcement was made. He was flabbergasted and immediately went into shock.

Barnes had been in charge of the Texas Division Research and Development, with an office in the W. R. Veazey Research Center. Beutel was to have his main office in Houston, but would also keep his office in Freeport for a time. Beutel wanted Barnes to move into the office next to him, and this involved other executive moves that raised some eyebrows.

For the first six months while Barnes was getting his feet on the ground in the new job, the organization Beutel had built carried on, and the transition was actually being made rather well. However, in September, Hurricane Carla came on the scene. After working through this crisis, Barnes felt he was really and truly the general manager of the Texas Division.

The hurricane was still out in the Gulf on a Thursday. Beutel was getting ready to go to Midland, Michigan, for a meeting, and the weather here was beautiful. On Friday, Beutel left for the weekend. Joe Tod, the general manager's chief of staff, said it was essential that a decision be made about a shutdown since the storm was getting closer.

Barnes said they didn't want to shut down if it were at all possible not to do so. He called a meeting of the major managers for Saturday at 9 a.m. That day clouds were starting a circular motion and stormy conditions were increasing. It was decided to shut down. The written plan for shutdown, which included the magnesium and chlorine cells, called for a shutdown period of eight hours. However, three hours later, maintenance major manager Shorkey walked in and handed Barnes a car key, saying he might want to use the car during the storm. Shorkey said everything was down but the power houses.

This was the beginning of chaos. Barnes got his family to Houston Saturday night and when he returned Sunday morning, water was coming over the Velasco bridge and leaking into Plant A through the Ethyl Dow intake flume. Water was so high at Plant A that Jack Turner was concerned for his power crews there. It was finally decided to shut down the power plant and evacuate his people.

Turner thought the decision also called for shutdown of the Plant B power plant. However, he was told that B's power should be left on. If the Houston Lighting and Power tieline went down, they would not be able to get Power B started again. Turner caught the crews at the B stockroom on their way out, and sent them back to the power house. There they started to fire up the boiler to be ready to start the power generators. However, by 10 p.m. Sunday night the winds tore down the Houston Lighting and Power tieline, thus eliminating the start-up source.

On Monday morning, water was coming into Plant B. It actually came around the levee and flooded Clute, Lake

DR. EARLE B. BARNES

Jackson and Plant B. As Barnes, Shorkey, Roush, Turner, and others were trying to figure out how to start Power B, W. F. English of the Fire Department, and Bobby Freeman of the Power Department, had a great idea. They could hook up the fire engine hoses to the boiler feed and, using the fire engine pump, get water to the boilers. Then, English said that with the 90-mile-per-hour winds at the top of the stack, they should have enough draft to light the boilers without the use of blower fans.

They decided to try it. The fire engines were hooked up, the boiler was lit off and in a short time they had steam. Then the generators could be steam-driven to put Power B back in operation.

Hurricane Carla swamped both Plants A and B, and it took until the end of October before they were running again. It involved the whole Texas Division to get them going, and this made Earle Barnes feel like this was now his organization as he began his five eventful years as general manager.

197

45

Good PR
Helps After Explosion

J. M. (LEVI) Leathers, general manager of Dow's Texas Division from January 1967 till October 1968 tells of several memorable events during his administration. His new responsibility had been announced in October 1966, and the happening occurred just before Christmas of 1966. He actually took over the general manager's job on that day.

An explosion occurred during mixing of a special agricultural product for Dow Sales. The mixing was done at the plant in tank car lots, as a courtesy to the Sales Department, so the customer would not need to mix it in the field. As a precautionary measure, the mixing was done in the back end of the plant away from other production units. Unfortunately, one chemical was shock sensitive, and due to some sort of shock in the mixing process, it set off a major explosion which involved some fatalities.

Levi and his public relations director, Bill Boddie, decided they would allow full press and photo coverage as soon as it was safe for press representatives to approach the scene in order to avoid bad press coverage. This had recently occurred in Houston when a different chemical company had an accident and wouldn't give out any information. Consequently, the open position of Dow at Freeport with the press was reported in both the local and Houston papers as a great public service.

Another important event that occurred during Leathers' administration was the creation of the Oyster Creek Division of Dow, which Levi had pushed as a new concept in chemical manufacturing. It was the use of fully integrated plants to produce basic chemicals, using the latest technology at the lowest possible cost, and the building of huge world-scale plants. Salaried technicians were responsible for maintaining and operating the plants, which reduced costs through improved manpower utilization.

One integrated plant was Vinyl Chloride, with the first unit producing 700 million pounds per year of product. It was an integrated plant because Ethylene Dichloride was cracked to make Vinyl Chloride and a by-product (HCl). The HCl was then reacted with air and Ethylene, to make more Ethylene Dichloride, which was recycled for cracking to make more Vinyl Chloride. The plant was balanced so that all by-product (HCl) was used to make more Ethylene Dichloride.

The other product was Chlorine-Caustic. It had its own power source and its own chlorine cells to separate the chlorine and caustic. It produced 1,000 tons a day of chlorine.

The third occasion which stands out for Levi occurred when the Texas Division passed five million man hours without a lost time accident and received the President's Award. Ted Doan, president of Dow Chemical Co., came to Texas and made the award.

*

David Rooke was the general manager of the Texas Division from 1968 to 1973. He recalls the time he decided the Division wasn't doing enough in support of the community and the community leadership. He appointed a special group of men and assigned them to work with local government officials, church and school leaders, business and professional people, and leaders of all kinds. This group included Nig Raney, Herman Swift, Rufus Brewer, Wade Lorenz, Gene Morgan, Jim Cope and Bill Colegrove.

DAVID ROOKE   **J. M. "LEVI" LEATHERS**

It was the responsibility of this special group to personally contact individuals and groups to ensure that these leaders understood more about Dow, its philosophy, its current operations, and its plans for the future. To further the same objective, Rooke continued to give an annual report to the community, which had been originated by Barnes and continued by Leathers.

These annual reports were given for several years during the Rooke administration. He spent a considerable amount of time in an attempt to put together a program that would be interesting to the people and, let them know what the company's future looked like at that time. The reports were presented to thousands of local citizens at the high school auditorium. Rooke said, "How can you expect support from the community if they don't know what you are doing?"

Safety was very high in Rooke's priorities. Barnes and Leathers had taken top manufacturing executives and given them each a tour of two or three years as Division safety director. Rooke went even further by asking each of his major managers to take one of the manager's key people and place him full time for a year as safety director in the major manager's department. This meant that safety was headed up by people capable of pushing safety and getting results in every department of the Division.

Rooke has the deep down feeling that the community of Brazosport and the state of Texas still have the best climate in the United States for building and operating chemical plants. The reason is that people of this community and state expect chemical plants to be first class citizens, but on the other hand, they support chemical plants with services, with personal actions, laws, attitudes, and government positions which make the community and state first class in turn. This is important when companies go to locate in a place, and influences why they stay and grow.

Rooke is impressed by the strength of the people in the Texas Division, whether responding to a business downturn or, when business is good, making the extra pounds, or responding to environmental concerns. If a plant is needed in another part of the world, even with a different culture, the Texas Division people can go there and get the job done.

I end this report of David Rooke with his famous ratchet philosophy. He says, "Today's best performance is only a minimal, acceptable performance for tomorrow. There is only one way to go and that is up."

46

Texas & Louisiana Divisions Differ

EVERETT "JAKE" Jacob was general manager of Dow's Texas Division from 1973 to 1977. He came to the Texas Division after serving as general manager for several years at Dow's Louisiana Division. In comparing the Louisiana and Texas Divisions of Dow, Jacob refers to the Louisiana Division as a "Teen Age" plant, and the Texas Division as a "Middle Age" plant. This, of course, refers to the ages of the two organizations, as well as their sizes.

Coming to Texas brought Jacob in contact with 7,000 employees of a much larger Division. It took several months of weekly dinner meetings just to become personally acquainted with his superintendents. Being larger, the Texas Division also had more protocol than the Louisiana group.

Jacob actually felt lost in Dr. Beutel's old office in the administration building. It was an extremely large room with the free-form table Beutel had used for so many years. Jacob decided to divide the large room into smaller offices, and asked Levi Leathers, his boss in Michigan, if it would be okay to do so. Leathers said, "We had better check with Earle Barnes (Leathers' boss) to see if it will be all right."

Barnes replied, "Absolutely okay, Jake; if you want your office outside in a wooden shack, you can have it there." So the big office was cut down somewhat, and a small conference room, a major manager's office, and a secretary's office were added.

Jacob remembers well the first and only annual stockholders' meeting of the Dow Chemical Co. held in Freeport, which occurred during his administration. The Board of Directors wanted to hold a meeting in the Southwest, but were afraid the Freeport facilities would be too small. They tried to set it up in Houston, but the date conflicted with the Offshore Technology Conference, which used up just about all the hotel rooms in Houston.

So the meeting was held in Freeport after all. Most of the Holiday Inn was taken over for the out-of-town folks, and the high school auditorium was used for the stockholders' meeting. One barbeque was put on at the Lake Jackson Pavilion for non-Dow community leaders, and another for Dow supervisors and their wives. All the Dow directors and their wives stood in a receiving line under the trees at the park and greeted the guests. Jacob said his staff performed admirably, and the whole affair went off smoothly and efficiently, resulting in letters of commendation from top Dow officials.

Another memorable event during Jacob's administration was the opening of the new Fine Arts Center. This project was started by David Rooke when he was general manager, and was helped tremendously by large donations from the Dow Chemical Co. and the Rollin Gerstacker Foundation. In addition, healthy financial support was given by the community. This beautiful and useful center has enhanced the quality of life in this area.

*

Don Rikard was general manager of the Texas Division from January 1977 till May 1978. He was impressed by the amount of time the general manager had to spend on non-manufacturing matters, such as employee relations, government affairs, community relations, safety, and in general, people relations of all kinds. This takes a majority of the general manager's time.

Rikard says the strength of the Texas Division is the basic foundation of a lot of highly qualified, ambitious, aggressive people who make the Division what it is. We are going to need more people like these in the future, he says, because while we still have good transportation, both by land and water, other benefits which were present in the early days, like low cost hydrocarbons, will be no more. It will take involved, creative people in order to beat the rest of the world.

Rikard told me his job as general manager of the Texas Division was absolutely the best job he ever had.

*

H. H. McClure has been general manager of the Texas Division from 1978 to the present. He vividly recalls the heavy rains of 1979 when 26 inches of rain fell in 24 hours, causing what was termed a "100-year flood."

The most heavily threatened plants were in Dow's North Process Area at Plant A, where the rains inside the levee put the Jumbo EDC and Chlorine 6 Plants in danger from high water. Coupled with this was the threat outside the North Process Area levee from high water, due to the heavy drainage from the Clute-Lake Jackson area. Dirt was added to raise that levee, and still the water came within a foot of the top. Fortunately, there was only a modest tide so the natural drainage through the high East Storm Protection levee was reasonably fast and the strengthened North Process Area levee held.

The torrential rains did cause a cutback in Chlorine 6 because the water level came close to the switchgear. Also, pumps were flooded around some storage tanks in that area. The Dorr Plant area in Plant A had to be shut down temporarily. Nothing serious happened in Plant B, but the expense of downtime and property damage at both plants amounted to about $3 million. To give you an idea how often a "100-year flood" may come, about three months later there was another torrential rain causing a "100-year flood" condition again.

The second highlight McClure recalls occurred in November

1981. It was the gift of 25 acres of land at the old Lake Jackson Airport to the Community Hospital, as a site for a new hospital. Additionally, Dow paid $3 million to the Hospital Board for the old hospital building and donated another $5.5 million to be used for capital needs through June 1985.

McClure had been working with the Hospital Board for three or four years to help find a new location for it. Expansion of the Dow plants and growth of the local communities had made it necessary to move the hospital from the Plant B area. Again we see evidence of an important gift from Dow to the Brazosport community.

Upper left:
EVERETT JACOB
GM 1973-1977

Upper Right:
DON RICKARD
GM 1977-1978

Lower Left:
H. H. McCLURE
Present GM

47

'60s Saw
New General Managers

DOW TEXAS Division's original general manager, Dr. A. P. Beutel, was honored for 50 years of service with Dow in November 1966, at a testimonial dinner given at the Warwick Hotel in Houston. Southern leaders in the fields of education, finance, and industry were part of the program honoring this "builder of both men and organizations, of chemical plants, and business enterprises." He was also saluted as the "pioneering personality of the chemical industry in the Southwest."

It was in December of that year that Levi Leathers became general manager of the Texas Division. Dr. Earle B. Barnes was moved up to Corporate Director of Manufacturing, Engineering and Maintenance.

*

The Dow Oyster Creek Division at Freeport was announced in 1967, with R. T. Johnson as general manager. This Division was created in order to produce basic chemicals at the lowest possible cost, by using the latest technology and building large world-scale plants. Salaried technicians were responsible for maintaining and operating the plants, which reduced costs through improved manpower utilization. The first two products of the Oyster Creek Division were to be Vinyl Chloride and Chlorine-Caustic.

Also in 1967, a new plastic airplane made from Dow materials was completed. It was called the "Windecker Eagle I," named after the inventor. Leo Windecker and his wife, Fairfax, had both been well-known dentists in Lake Jackson.

*

During April of 1968, several single Dow employees set up a one-shot, computer-selected date system. Singles would fill out an application and send it to Zahia Tabatabai of Industrial Relations, who was the coordinator. Applications were to be in by Friday, August 23. The computer, which was set to discard any married applicants, would then select couples for a date.

Levi Leathers was promoted to Director of Operations for the U. S. area of Dow in 1968. David Rooke became general manager of the Texas Division.

DOW MATERIALS—Pilot Bill Lowery climbs aboard the Windecker Eagle I, a plastic airplane constructed of Dow materials and designed by a Lake Jackson dentist. Its initial flights were events of 1968 in Brazosport.

In 1970, a group of Texas Division employees sponsored a chartered jet flight to Europe, costing $310 round trip per person, a very reasonable cost. While in Europe, they were on their own and could go to cities of their choice, providing they were back to the departure city on time to catch the charter flight home.

During June of 1970, a research project involving the raising of catfish was conducted by Dow's Agricultural Research Laboratory in Dow's Brazoria Reservoir. Those fishing in the reservoir were elated as they began to catch big strings of catfish, even though the object of the project was to raise catfish for the commercial market.

*

As this series approaches its end, I want to tell you about a fellow that I call a "character," because he is one of a kind and probably better known to more people than most any other Dow employee. I am referring to E. A. "Scotty" Scott, who, with his ever-present cigar, has probably prepared more barbeque than anyone else you could think of.

One day while preparing for a fancy barbeque, the meat that had been ordered didn't arrive. At 9 a.m. on the day of the event, "Scotty" selected some top sirloin butts which were on hand for roasts at the Dow cafeteria. After pulling all the tricks he knew to get the meat prepared in time, it came out "perfect." Dr. Beutel said it was such good barbeque that from then on it would be the standard meat for all barbeques.

"Scotty" came to this area to work for Dow Security in 1946. He had to rent a chicken coop in Clute to live in temporarily. After eight or nine months, he bought a house in Clute, and then in the '50s bought his present home just across the railroad tracks on the old Angleton highway.

He started out doing barbeques helping Red Smitherman, who was also in Plant Security. "Scotty" did a number of barbeques with Smitherman, and then branched out on his own, making certain changes and improvements he developed himself. Many remember "Scotty" for his specialty of barbequed shrimp. He used his own special sauce and says these shrimp are like peanuts—once you start eating them, you can't stop.

Most of his jobs were for Dow groups, but he did cook for

others like the Girls' Softball teams, DeMolay, Eastern Star, etc. "Scotty" was even called several times to the LBJ Ranch near Johnson City to help put on barbeques for President Lyndon Johnson. The largest barbeque "Scotty" ever did was an American Legion Barbeque where he prepared for 7,500 people. He used two Dow barbeque pits and four temporary pits in the Brazosport area. He supervised the six pits and served the food in the Dow Pavilion with 26 helpers.

As a member of the Brazoria County Chuckwagon Gang, "Scotty" has prepared barbeque as far away as Tyler. The Brazoria County Press and Radio Parties were known far and wide, and featured each year "Scotty's" wonderful barbequed shrimp. I helped put on a barbeque for John Connally at the Brazoria County Fairgrounds where "Scotty" did the barbeque. We served 3,500 people at 10 double lines in the auditorium. His last big job was at the Dow plant in Russellville, Arkansas, in 1981, where he fed 1,060 people in 27 minutes.

"Scotty" is now retired from Dow and many of us have bought wood for our fireplaces from his big woodyard near his home. He still does a few barbeques and fish frys to keep in practice. For instance, one party for the Angleton Masonic Lodge involved an oyster fry and 50 gallons of oyster stew.

"Scotty," you are one of a kind!

**DOW'S
E. A.
"SCOTTY"
SCOTT**

48

Super Tanker Launched in '71

A NEW super tanker for Dow was launched in July 1971. It was christened the *S. S. Marine Chemist,* and replaced Dow's old *Marine Chemist.*

The original general manager of Dow's Texas Division, Dr. A. P. Beutel, retired from the company at the age of 78, after serving 55 years with Dow. He had joined the company on April 29, 1916. At the time of his retirement, Carl A. Gerstacker, chairman of the board, conferred the life title of "Director Emeritus" on Beutel.

March marked the start of a weekly tour service at the Dow plants, using six women employees as guides, dressed in special uniforms and pillbox hats. The tour was given every Monday afternoon, and the women took turns being the guides. Dow received many compliments concerning the tours.

A Plant B vegetable garden, complete with beans, peppers, okra, squash, cucumbers, radishes, zinnias, sunflowers, bachelor buttons, roses, azaleas, and kumquats, was shown near Gate 38. The garden was planted in order to prove that plants would grow in the area near the chemical complex.

In November 1972, Jim Case became editor of the *DOW TEXAN.* He was later promoted to director of public relations for Dowell in its Houston headquarters.

Dr. A. P. Beutel died on November 27, 1972, two weeks after his 80th birthday.

David Rooke, general manager of the Texas Division, was moved to corporate headquarters in Midland, Michigan, in October 1973, as vice president of Supply and Distribution for Dow Chemical U.S.A., and Everett Jacob became general manager of the Texas Division.

Dun's Review of December 1975, named Dow one of the five best managed companies of 1975. Dow received the award for its sophisticated financial management. *Dun's* comments: "Others have called its financial management the most complex, sophisticated and sometimes daring financial operations inside any U. S. industrial company."

On January 21, 1976, Dow observed the 35th anniversary of the dipping of the first ingot of magnesium from the sea. Three of the original group were still working: Jordan Mariam, Floyd Honeycutt, and Leo (Bailey) Hellman. Retirees who were present and still living in the area were David Landsborough and Lee Hellums.

In July 1976, Bill Colegrove, manager of Texas Division Community Relations, received the President's Award from the Beautify Texas Council. The Council paid tribute to Dow Chemical U.S.A. for supporting the work and duties Colegrove performed on behalf of the Beautify Texas Council since its founding.

*

Continuing what I began in a prior episode, I want to tell you about another "character." This one is the great Dow "chef extraordinaire," L. E. "Chubby" Lamb.

I met "Chubby" for the first time on the Friday before the first day of October 1945. I was in charge of Dow's Plant A cafeteria, and we were in a terrible jam for a cook when "Chubby" walked in. I asked him to start work that night, but he begged off until the following Monday so he could go to Houston and get his wife.

On Sunday, September 30, he and his wife came down riding in a cattle truck with bucket seats, which was the Continental

Trailways Bus Service at that time from Houston to Freeport. The ride took four hours, and they stopped at nearly every mailbox along the way. "Chubby" started work on Monday, and it was the beginning of a long and pleasant relationship with him.

He had begun work at age 17 as a dishwasher and cook's helper in a restaurant near the Shell Refinery in Deer Park. He went from there to San Diego as a fry cook in his brother's restaurant, where he would fry 1,000 hamburgers a day on an

L. E. "CHUBBY" LAMB

enormous grill. "Chubby" graduated to dinner cook in San Diego and then enlisted in the Navy as a third-class cook. He cooked at Corpus Christi and Kingsville Naval Stations. Later he was transferred to Receife in Brazil and upgraded to first class cook and chief commissary steward.

After joining Dow, "Chubby" worked at the Plant A Cafeteria, and later at the Dow Hotel as chef. Still later, he ran the old Dow Lodge, about a quarter of a mile from the present Dow Plantation House. In the beginning, parties were usually small with eight to 10 guests. He would buy the groceries, cook and serve the food, and tend bar on the side.

In 1961, "Chubby" was in charge of food at the Brazoria Reservoir, as well as of food operations at the Lodge. He worked many interesting and beautiful parties at the Dow Lodge. One of the parties had a theme, "Around the World." Recipes were used from Scandinavia, Holland, Germany, France, England, Italy, Greece, India, Hawaii, China, Mexico, and the United States. The buffet table had to be redesigned with a second tier above the table top in order to display all the various foods.

I recall one party "Chubby" handled when Dr. Earle B. Barnes moved from Texas to Midland, Michigan. He used 120 beef tenderloins which were charcoaled on the barbeque pit at the pavilion. The meat supplier said this was the most tenderloins he had ever sold at one time.

In 1974, the Dow Plantation House was built near where the old Dow Lodge used to be. "Chubby" was put in charge of food preparation, and as always, did an excellent job.

"Chubby" is the best all-around cook I know of. He can prepare small quantities for a party of four to six people, or prepare great quantities to serve several thousand. At least twice, he has been called all the way up to Midland, Michigan, to put on an authentic Texas barbeque for the Dow people up there.

DOW TOUR SERVICE—Uniformed guides lined up by the bus when a new plant tour service was begun in 1971.

Final Episode

AND NOW, 11 months since I started these stories about Dow and the Brazosport communities and people, it is time to draw them to a close.

I retired from Dow on January 31, 1977, after 41½ years of exciting and rewarding service with Dow. My memories extend back to 1935 in Midland, Michigan, when I worked for Dr. E. C. Britton, director of Organic Research, and on to work with Dr. Beutel who was assistant general manager of Dow and general manager of the Texas Division.

After that I worked with Bill Boddie who taught me just about all I know of public and community relations. Later my supervisors were Joe Tod, Ray Brubaker, Luther Evans, David Rooke and Bob Bryant, all outstanding Dow executives.

After retirement, Jim Nabors, Glenn Heath, and my editor, Roberta Dansby, helped me to become a writer.

To all you readers who have been interested in these reminiscences of early Texas Dow, it is time to say, "Thank You!"

bill colegrove

Sena and Bill Colegrove are donating all of the royalties and proceeds from the sale of this Limited Edition to the Lake Jackson Historical Association.

ABOUT THE AUTHOR

William D. Colegrove was born in Remus, Michigan in 1912, the son of William D. Colegrove, Sr., and Carrie Hoyt Colegrove. His father was owner of a general store there and later became Postmaster.

He grew up in Remus (population 600), and graduated from high school with the distinction of being the youngest valedictorian in Michigan that year.

He earned a degree in Electrical Engineering in 1931 from what is now Michigan State University.

Not long after graduation he joined The Dow Chemical Company in Midland, Michigan as Secretary to Dr. E. C. Britton, the Director of Organic Research.

In 1937 he was made Secretary to Dr. A. P. Beutel, Assistant General Manager of The Dow Chemical Company.

He came to Texas with Beutel in 1940 as the Dow complex was just starting in Freeport. During his 42 years with Dow, he served in numerous executive and managerial capacities with the hospital, cafeteria, housing, and other departments.

Working with Beutel, he became familiar with the wide sweep of the company, and with the multitude of details involved in tying it together. He gained a broader acquaintance than virtually anyone at Dow, particularly with those outside the company.

From 1948 to 1954, he served as Mayor of the City of Lake Jackson.

In 1953 he was chosen by the Brazosport Chamber of Commerce as the Outstanding Citizen of Brazosport.

In 1978 the United Way, in recognition of his outstanding community contributions, established **"The William D. Colegrove Award,"** to be awarded annually, using his standards of community service as a guideline for those individuals selected to receive it.

After retirement in 1977, he became Director of Marketing for the Angleton Bank of Commerce , and for a while was a columnist for the Brazosport Facts newspaper.

He and his wife, Sena, celebrated their 53rd wedding anniversary in 1988.

THE END